Uncle Sam and You

Student Workbook

Notgrass company

Uncle Sam and You
Student Workbook
by John Notgrass and Charlene Notgrass

The activities in this book review information learned in the daily lessons of *Uncle Sam and You*. After your child reads a lesson in *Uncle Sam and You,* he should complete the activity in this book that corresponds to that lesson. At the end of each unit, he may take the optional test. The questions on each test are drawn primarily from the activities in the workbook.

ISBN 978-1-60999-053-4

Printed in the United States of America.

Notgrass Company
975 Roaring River Road
Gainesboro, TN 38562

1-800-211-8793
www.notgrass.com

Welcome Home

Write the letter that is in front of each church name at the top of the page in the blank beside the description that matches it at the bottom of the page.

A. Auburn University Chapel (Auburn, Alabama)

B. Trinity Episcopal Church (Independence, Missouri)

C. St. Peter's Episcopal Church (Seward, Alaska)

D. Grace United Methodist Church (Harrisburg, Pennsylvania)

E. 16th and Decatur Church of Christ (Washington, D.C.)

F. Maranatha Baptist Church (Plains, Georgia)

G. Grace Episcopal Church (Galveston, Texas)

_____ This is the home church of Jimmy and Rosalynn Carter.

_____ A painting by Dutch artist Jan Van Emple is located here.

_____ This church building was built with bricks made by slaves.

_____ This church building survived a hurricane.

_____ Congressman Joe L. Evins attended this congregation.

_____ A state legislature met in this church building after a fire destroyed the capitol.

_____ Harry and Bess Truman were married here in 1919.

St. Peter's Episcopal Church, Seward, Alaska

Fifty States One Nation I

Using information in lesson 2, color states 1-13 red; color states 14-17 green, and color states 18-29 blue.

Fifty States One Nation II

Step 1: Unscramble the eleven states of the Confederacy. See page 15 in the text.
Step 2: On the student workbook map for Lesson 2 and on the maps of Alaska and Hawaii below, color states 30-33 yellow; color states 34-36 brown; and color states 37-50 orange. Use information in Lesson 3.

SUTOH COANRILA ____________________

MSIPSISPSII ____________________

FDIROLA ____________________

AMBLAAA ____________________

GOGRIEA ____________________

LUOIIANSA ____________________

TAXES ____________________

VNGIIIRA ____________________

ASANRAKS ____________________

NTROH COANRILA ____________________

TSEENESNE ____________________

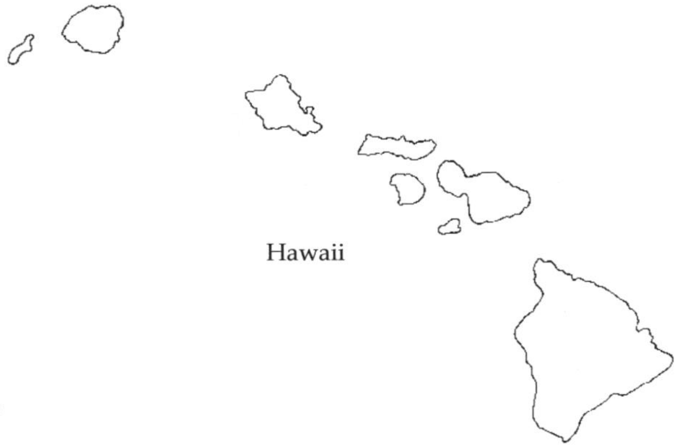

Lesson 4

Out of Many, One

New words have come into English from many other languages. Under each picture below, write the name of the language from which the English word comes. You will use each language from the list once. Look at the blue boxes on pages 24-25 in the text if you need help.

Mikmac	**Inuit**	**Narragansett**	**Italian**
Spanish	**Dutch**	**French**	**German**
Norwegian	**Turkish**	**Yiddish**	**Malay**

canyon

bagel

caribou

garage

kayak

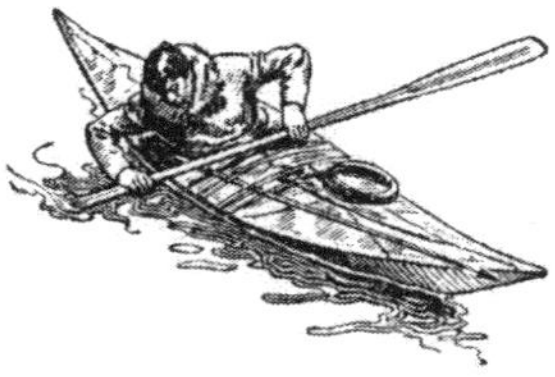

cookie

yogurt

ski

hamburger

gingham

balcony

squash

Take the test for Unit 1 on page 121.

The National Archives

Draw a line from each statement on the left to the correct match on the right. To find some answers, you will need to look at photos in the lesson.

1.	He spoke at the opening of the Emancipation Proclamation Exhibit in 1963.	•	• **Herbert Hoover**
2.	He designed the statues called "The Past" and "The Future" outside the National Archives.	•	• **120**
3.	In its display at the National Archives, the Declaration of Independence is written on this many sheets of parchment.	•	• **Barry Faulkner**
4.	He laid the cornerstone for the National Archives in 1933.	•	• **Robert Kennedy**
5.	The number of staff members who first worked at the National Archives in 1935.	•	• **Robert I. Aitken**
6.	He painted the two murals at the National Archives called "The Declaration" and "The Constitution."	•	• **4**
7.	In its display at the National Archives, the Constitution is written on this many sheets of parchment.	•	• **1**
8.	Four of the statues outside the National Archives were carved from limestone blocks weighing this many tons each.	•	• **125**

Lesson 7

The Declaration of Independence

Complete the timeline of the Declaration of Independence by filling in these blanks with these words:

Benjamin Franklin **British** **Continental Congress**
independence **parchment** **draft** **final** **approves**

Sept. - Oct. 1774	The ____________________ ____________________ meets in Philadelphia.
April 1775	Battles between _____________ soldiers and colonists at Lexington and Concord in Massachusetts.
June 7, 1776	Richard Henry Lee makes a motion that the colonies declare their __________________ from Great Britain.
June 11, 1776	The Continental Congress gives the task of writing reasons for the independence of the colonies to Thomas Jefferson, John Adams, Roger Sherman, __________________ __________________, and Robert Livingston.
June 28, 1776	The first __________________ of the declaration is presented to the Continental Congress.
July 2, 1776	The Continental Congress ____________________ Richard Henry Lee's motion.
July 4, 1776	The Continental Congress approves the ___________ version of the Declaration of Independence.
August 2, 1776	Most members signed the __________________ copy of the Declaration of Independence.

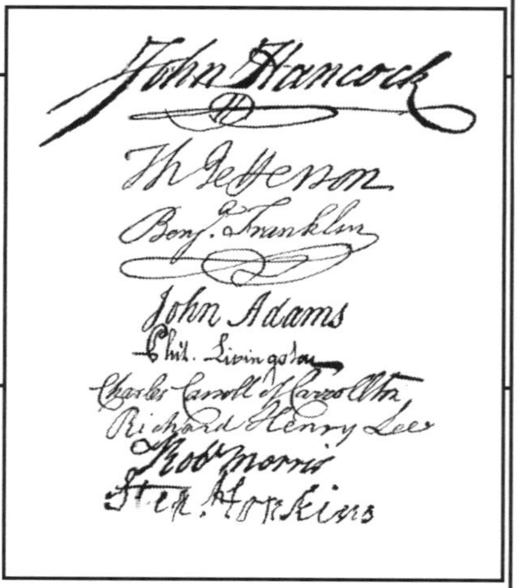

Signatures from the Declaration

The United States Constitution

In the Preamble to the Constitution below, find each word that is in ALL CAPS. Write each of these words on the line in the puzzle where it fits.

We the **PEOPLE** of the United **STATES**, in Order to form a more perfect **UNION**, establish **JUSTICE**, insure domestic **TRANQUILITY**, provide for the **COMMON DEFENCE**, promote the general Welfare, and **SECURE** the **BLESSINGS** of **LIBERTY** to ourselves and our **POSTERITY**, do ordain and establish this Constitution for the United States of **AMERICA**.

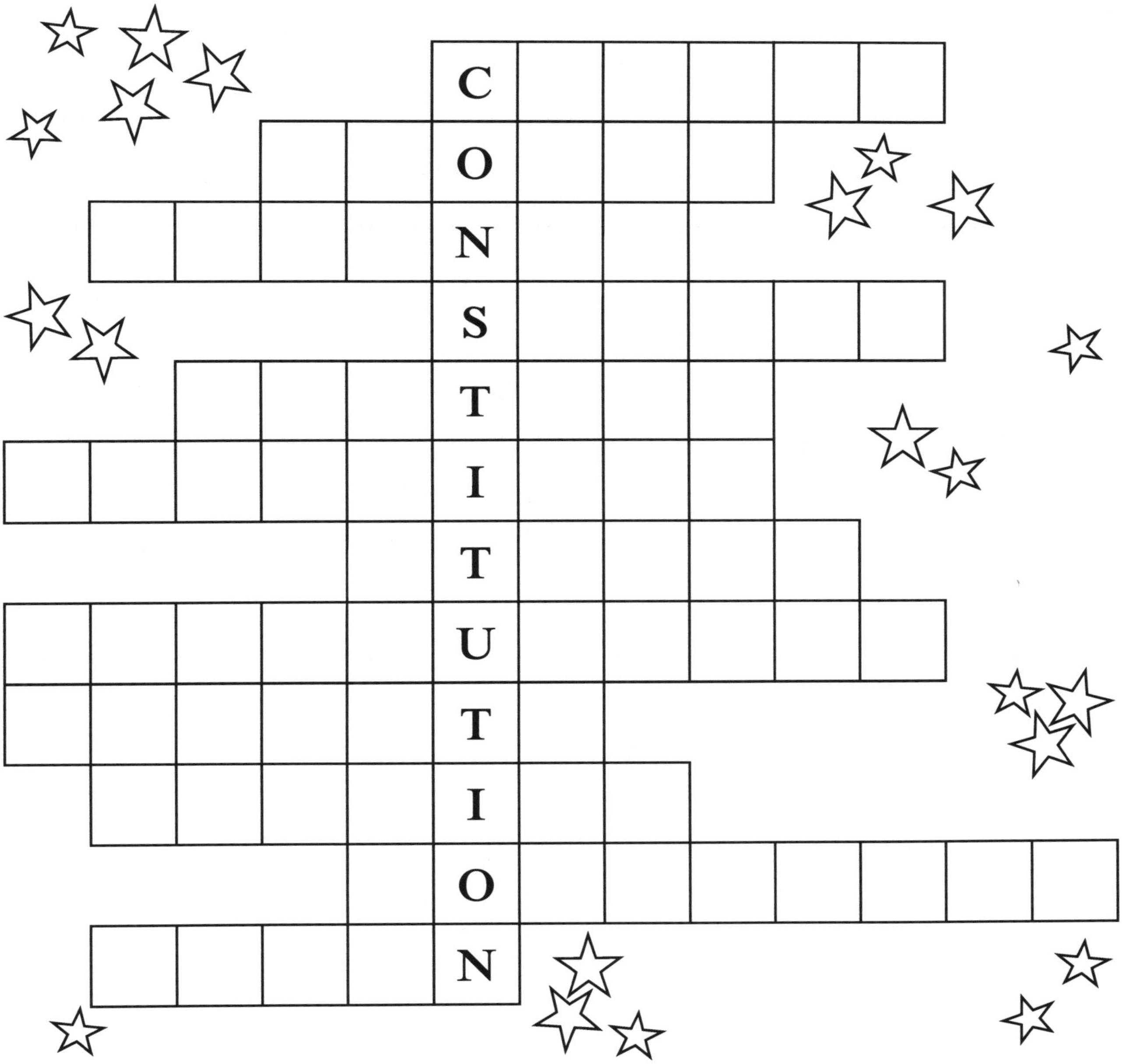

Lesson 9

The Bill of Rights

Complete this crossword puzzle using information from the Bill of Rights.

Across

1. Congress cannot prohibit the free exercise of what?
3. Who cannot be quartered in private homes without the owner's permission?
5. Without due process of law, no one can be deprived of life, liberty, or what?
7. In common law cases, people have the right to a trial by what?
9. The Constitution enumerates certain what?

Down

2. Americans have the right to keep and bear what?
4. What require probable cause to be issued?
6. Accused people have the right to a speedy and public what?
8. What shall not be required in excessive amounts?
10. Powers not given to the Federal government are reserved to the states and whom?

Take the test for Unit 2 on page 122.

Government on Three Levels

Draw the outline of your state. Draw a star to mark the location of your state capital and write its name beside the star. Draw a square to mark the location of your town and write its name beside the square.

Government in Three Branches

Follow the directions below to identify the correct match for each statement. Not all of the words at the bottom of the page will be used.

1. Draw a line under the name of the Frenchman who believed that government should be divided into three branches.

2. Draw a circle around the branch of the Federal government that passes laws.

3. Draw a diamond around the building in Philadelphia where all three branches of the Federal government met for a time.

4. Write a "1" beside the state that has a unicameral legislature.

5. Draw a square around the common name for a city executive.

Congress

Nebraska

mayor

Montesquieu

Burger

Federal Hall

Independence Hall

Supreme Court

Wisconsin

BIG CHEESE

America's Founding Fathers

Roger Sherman (1721-1793) was one of only two men to sign the Declaration of Independence, the Articles of Confederation, and the Constitution of the United States. In the puzzle below, find these words related to the life of Roger Sherman. All are horizontal or vertical.

Roger Sherman

CONNECTICUT	**ELIZABETH**
NEW HAVEN	**REBECCA**
YALE	**SERMONS**
MAYOR	**HONEST**
CONGRESS	**COMMITTEE**
REPRESENTATIVE	**SENATOR**

A	H	T	C	E	Y	B	T	U	E	E	U	V	X	Q	Z
R	W	T	O	Q	R	E	L	I	Z	A	B	E	T	H	E
E	S	E	N	A	T	O	R	C	S	B	E	W	X	Q	R
R	E	C	N	R	A	H	N	L	P	Y	N	R	W	X	E
E	R	R	E	R	W	F	C	O	M	M	I	T	T	E	E
B	W	V	C	F	D	V	O	E	B	Y	I	Y	E	D	V
E	W	R	T	R	W	G	N	E	W	H	A	V	E	N	R
C	X	B	I	F	D	F	G	W	Y	U	Y	T	B	E	W
C	R	T	C	B	C	X	R	E	V	R	W	E	R	W	E
A	Q	U	U	H	O	N	E	S	T	I	O	P	M	L	Y
D	F	B	T	Q	W	E	S	R	A	S	F	H	A	K	B
C	V	V	G	F	D	V	S	T	Z	X	D	G	Y	J	F
R	D	B	H	J	K	L	U	Y	S	E	R	M	O	N	S
Y	Y	A	L	E	P	O	I	M	N	C	V	B	R	A	W
F	U	T	R	U	O	K	J	P	B	V	S	E	R	Q	W
V	Y	R	E	P	R	E	S	E	N	T	A	T	I	V	E

Lesson 14

Uncle Sam Wants You

Use the following words to fill in the blanks below:

sacrifices hungry public
volunteering sick appointed
private juries

1. A pharmacist who owns his own drugstore works in the ______________ sector.

2. A pharmacist who works for a government-owned veterans hospital works in the ________________ sector.

3. People are not required to say yes when ______________ to a position, but our government needs people who are willing to serve.

4. America needs citizens who are willing to make the ____________________ necessary to be elected to various offices.

5. People who serve on ______________ are important to the American court system.

6. American citizens can make a positive impact by ______________________________.

7. In Matthew 25:35-36. Jesus talked about people who fed the _________________________.

8. Jesus also talked about people who visited the ______________.

Take the test for Unit 3 on page 123.

The Story of the Stars and Stripes

Circle the correct answer beneath each question.

1. When did the Marine Committee adopt the resolution describing the flag of the United States?

a. 1769 **b. 1801** **c. 1777**

2. How many stars and stripes did the flag of the United States have between 1794 and 1818?

a. fifteen **b. thirteen** **c. fifty**

3. Who led the team of seamstresses that made the flags for Fort McHenry?

a. Betsy Ross **b. Mary Pickersgill** **c. Martha Washington**

4. Which President signed the act of Congress making "The Star-Spangled Banner" our national anthem?

a. Herbert Hoover **b. Calvin Coolidge** **c. James Madison**

5. How many flags are displayed at the Avenue of Flags at Mount Rushmore?

a. ten **b. twenty-two** **c. fifty-six**

Lesson 17

The Great Seal of the United States

In this description of the Great Seal, find each word that is in ALL CAPS. Write each of these words on the line in the puzzle where it fits.

The Great Seal of the United States features an EAGLE protected by a SHIELD. The eagle is holding an OLIVE branch in one talon and thirteen ARROWS in the other. Above the eagle are thirteen STARS representing the thirteen original STATES. In the eagle's mouth is a ribbon with the phrase E PLURIBUS UNUM. On the back of the seal is a pyramid with an eye at the top and the phrase ANNUIT COEPTIS. The final design for the seal approved by Congress was submitted by CHARLES THOMSON.

More Treasured Symbols of America

Here are some patriotic song titles with the year each was written, published, or became significant in American history. Fill in each blank to complete the titles.

1767 ____________ Doodle

1831 ____________

1862 Battle __________ of the Republic

1879 __________ Father, Strong to Save

1895 America the ____________

1906 ____________ Aweigh

1908 The ___________ Go Rolling Along

1919 ____________ Hymn

1938 God ____________ America

1939 The U.S. ________ Force Song

American Ideals

Color the poster below in red and blue.

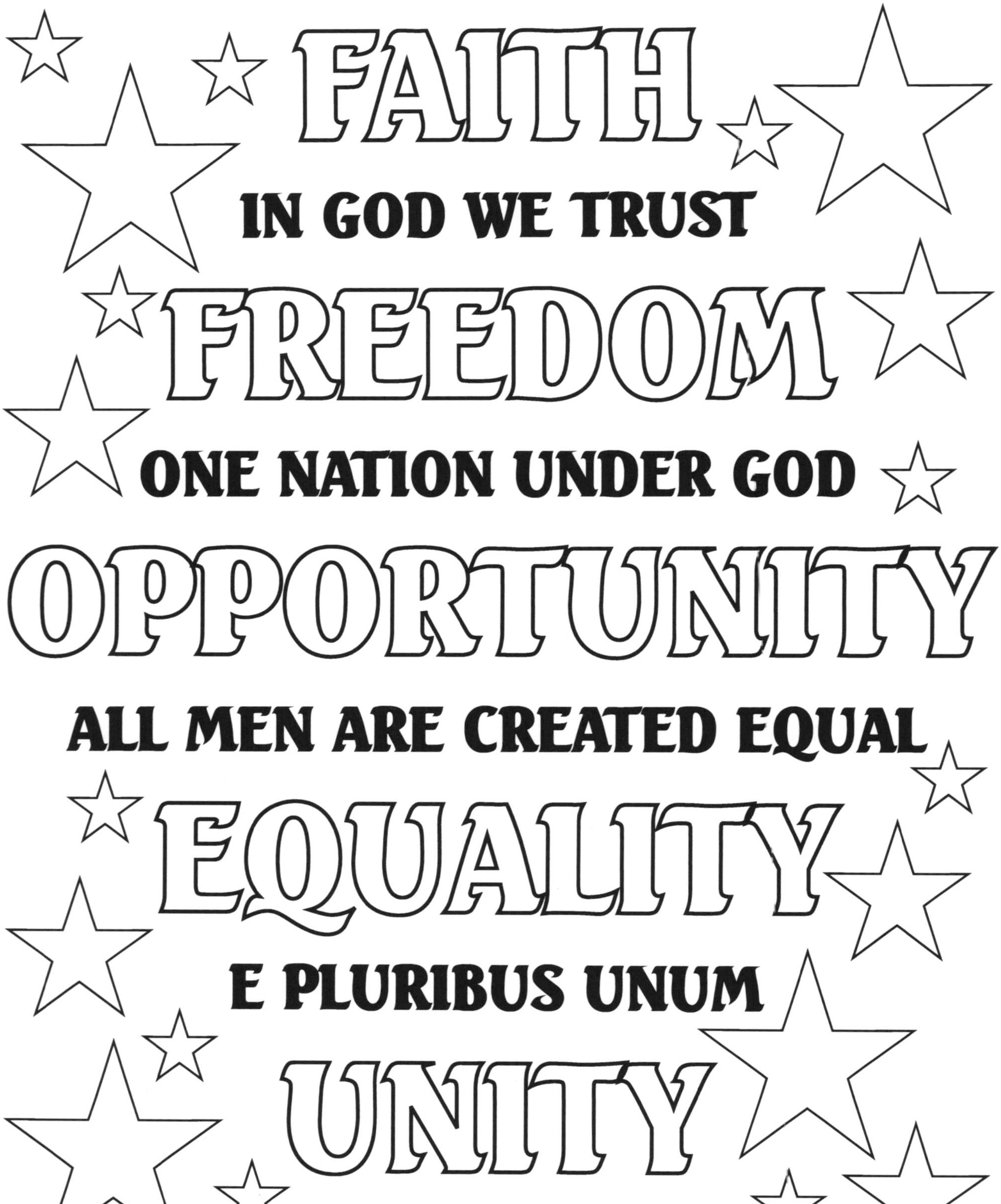

Take the test for Unit 4 on page 124.

Choosing People to Lead

Ask a parent if you need help finding the answers to these questions.

1. Who is the President of the United States?

____

2. Who are the two U.S. Senators from your state?

____

____

3. Who is the U.S. Representative from your district?

____

4. Who is the Governor of your state?

____

5. Who is your state senator in the state legislature?

____

6. Who is your state representative in the state legislature? (Residents of Nebraska will leave this blank.)

____

7. Who is chief executive in your city or county (may be called mayor, county executive, chief judge, or something else)?

____

Lesson 22

Presidents Make Peaceful Transitions

Complete this crossword puzzle using last names only.

Across

1. This President was inaugurated on January 21, 1985.
3. This President took his oath in Texas.
5. This President began the tradition of visiting the outgoing President before his Inauguration.
7. This President's inauguration was the first to be broadcast live on the Internet.
9. This President took his oath of office using a Dutch Bible.

Down

2. This President's inauguration was the first to be photographed.
4. This President was inaugurated for his only term in Philadelphia.
6. Gerald Ford became President after this President resigned.
8. This President's inauguration was the first to be broadcast on television.
10. This President's father administered his oath of office.

Presidents Theodore Roosevelt and William Howard Taft

Presidents' Home Sweet Homes

Using the information on the chart on page 119 of the text, follow the instructions below to color the map.

- Color red the states in which one President has been born.
- Color orange the states in which two Presidents have been born.
- Color yellow the states in which four Presidents have been born.
- Color green the state in which seven Presidents have been born.
- Color blue the state in which eight Presidents have been born.

Woodrow Wilson's Birthplace

Lesson 24

Presidential Birthdays and Families

Using the box on page 129 of the text, follow the directions below.

Draw an oval around the last names of the Presidents named Andrew.
Draw a line under the last names of the Presidents named Franklin.
Draw a diamond around the last names of the Presidents named George.
Draw a rectangle around the last names of the Presidents named James.
Draw a star above the last names of the Presidents named John.
Draw a line above the last names of the Presidents named Thomas.
Draw parentheses ( ) around the last names of the Presidents named William.

President Andrew Jackson

Adams

Taft

Carter

Coolidge

Bush

Harrison

Jackson

Clinton

Garfield

Bush

Tyler

Roosevelt

McKinley

Wilson

Pierce

Madison

Adams

Polk

Johnson

President Andrew Johnson

Buchanan

Washington

Jefferson

Kennedy

Monroe

Take the test for Unit 5 on page 125.

What Is Voting?

Write each word from the list on the correct blank to complete each sentence.

ballot	**referendum**	**candidate**
town meetings	**majority**	**voice vote**

1. If sixty people out of one hundred want something, they make a ____________________.

2. A vote by the people about a particular issue is called a _________________________.

3. Some small communities in New England still hold ______________________________.

4. A piece of paper that reflects a person's vote is called a ______________.

5. A person who is running for office is a ____________________.

6. When a group of people express their decision for or against an issue by speaking, it is called a ___________________________.

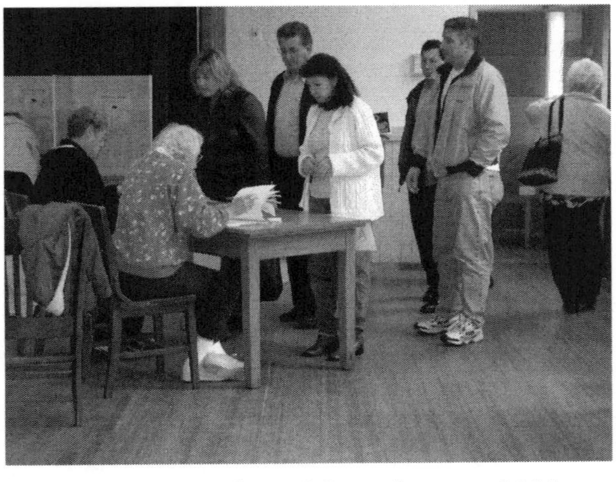

Voting in Boxboro, Massachusetts, 2006

Women Gain the Right to Vote

Maryland Woman in Voting Booth, 1944

In the puzzle below, find these words.

SUFFRAGE	**QUAKER**
MOTT	**STANTON**
ANTHONY	**EMERSON**
BEECHER	**WYOMING**
HOAR	**AMENDMENT**
RATIFY	**BURN**
CATT	**LEAGUE**

A	R	T	V	D	Y	B	Q	C	M	T	U	I	O	P	P
S	T	A	N	T	O	N	E	H	O	A	R	J	K	L	A
Z	X	C	V	S	B	N	M	A	T	Q	W	S	X	C	M
C	D	E	R	U	F	V	B	N	T	Y	H	U	I	O	E
K	M	N	H	F	Y	T	G	B	V	W	F	R	R	L	N
E	D	C	X	F	Z	A	Q	W	S	X	C	D	A	E	D
Q	B	U	I	R	T	W	E	Z	D	D	F	D	T	R	M
A	E	J	K	A	N	T	H	O	N	Y	G	V	I	F	E
Z	E	M	P	G	G	T	D	A	E	V	B	E	F	V	N
X	C	N	L	E	A	G	U	E	T	C	T	M	Y	G	T
C	H	H	O	H	R	R	D	E	F	X	Y	E	T	T	B
D	E	Y	L	Y	E	E	C	W	D	S	N	R	R	Y	H
E	R	T	I	N	Q	U	A	K	E	R	E	S	E	U	Y
R	B	G	K	M	D	T	T	D	W	E	V	O	C	J	I
F	V	B	U	J	F	R	T	F	B	U	R	N	E	N	U
W	Y	O	M	I	N	G	C	V	Q	W	W	W	Q	M	J

Minorities Gain the Right to Vote

Circle the correct answer beneath each question.

1. Which amendment to the U.S. Constitution stated that the right to vote could not be denied based on race, skin color, or former condition of servitude?

a. Thirteenth   b. Fourteenth   c. Fifteenth

2. What kind of test was required before people could vote in some places?

a. math test   b. science test   c. literacy test

3. What did the Twenty-fourth Amendment outlaw?

a. voting twice   b. poll taxes   c. campaign contributions

4. When did Congress pass the Indian Citizenship Act?

a. 1914   b. 1924   c. 1934

5. When did Congress pass the Manguson Act giving Chinese immigrants the right to become citizens and vote?

a. 1933   b. 1943   c. 1953

6. When did the Twenty-sixth Amendment take effect, giving eighteen-year-olds the right to vote?

a. 1971   b. 1981   c. 1991

Maryland Man Casts His Vote

Rules About Voting

Complete these sentences by filling in each blank with one of these choices:

register trustees district Tuesday
435 census precinct

North Dakota Voting Inspector, 1940

1. All federal elections are held on the first _____________ after the first Monday in November.

2. The United States is divided into ______ congressional districts.

3. Alaska, Delaware, Montana, North Dakota, South Dakota, Vermont, and Wyoming only have one congressional _________________ each.

4. The Federal government takes a ___________ every ten years.

5. The government officials in the Charter Township of West Bloomfield, Michigan, include clerk, supervisor, treasurer, and _______________.

6. A polling place is where the voters living in that _______________ come to vote.

7. To stop people from voting more than once, states require citizens

Take the test for Unit 6 on page 126

American Political Parties

Read this paragraph and put each word in ALL CAPS in its correct location in the puzzle below.

The **FEDERALIST** party flourished in the late 1700s. The **DEMOCRATIC-REPUBLICAN** party was strongest in the early 1800s. The **DEMOCRATIC** party developed in the 1820s, and the **WHIG** party followed in the 1830s. The **REPUBLICAN** party began in the 1850s. Several other parties existed in the late 1800s and early 1900s. In recent years, the **GREEN**, **CONSTITUTION**, and Libertarian parties have had a few candidates elected to local and state offices, but the Republicans and Democrats have been the two dominant parties since the mid-1800s.

Michigan State Republican Convention, 2010

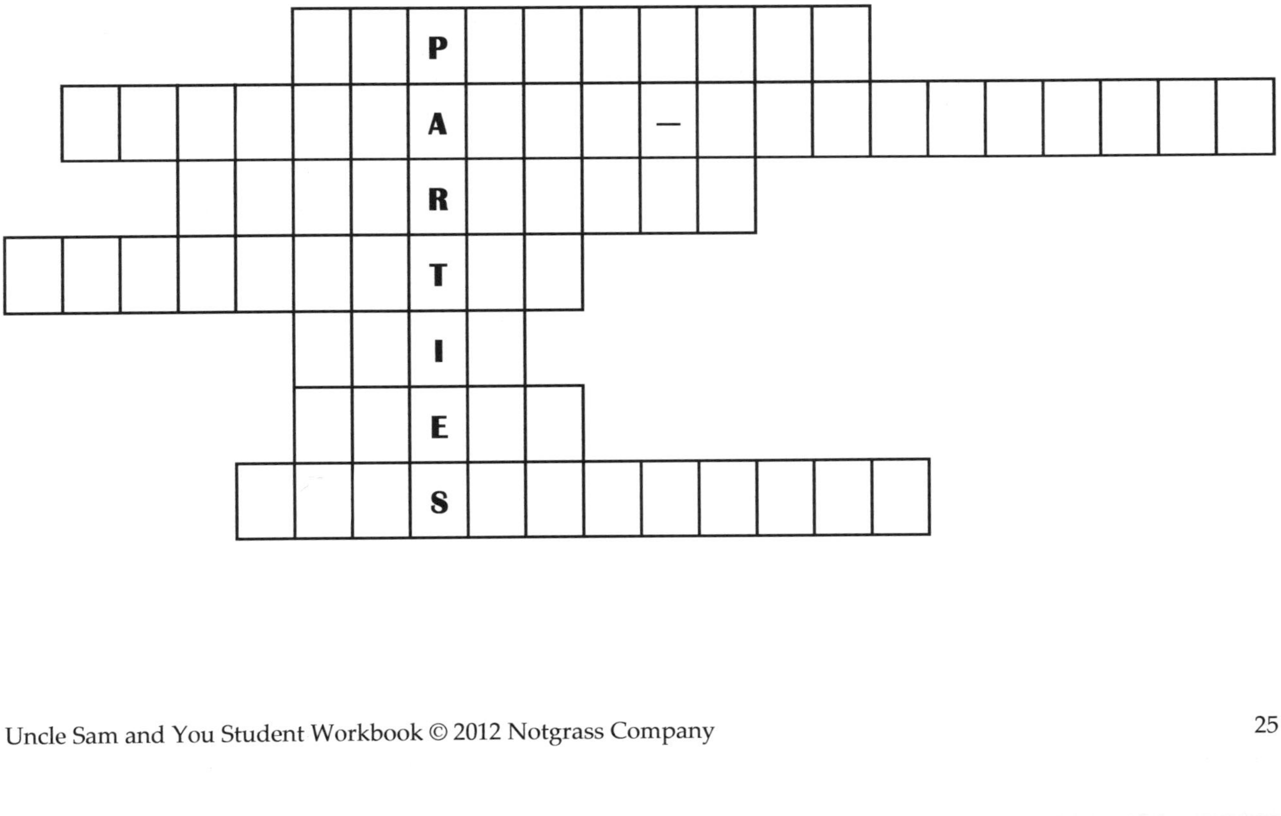

Lesson 32

Jumping Into the Race

The last names of five presidential candidates from 2004 to 2012 are hidden in the puzzle below. Find **CAIN** (2012), **PAWLENTY** (2012), **SANTORUM** (2012), **KERRY** (2004), and **BIDEN** (2008). Each of the rebus puzzles below also represent one of those names. Write the correct candidate beside each rebus.

A	P	A	W	L	E	N	T	Y	B	C	D	E	F	G	C	A	I	N	H
S	A	N	T	O	R	U	M	I	B	I	D	E	N	J	K	L	M	N	O
P	Q	R	S	K	E	R	R	Y	T	U	V	W	X	Y	Z	A	B	C	D

1. 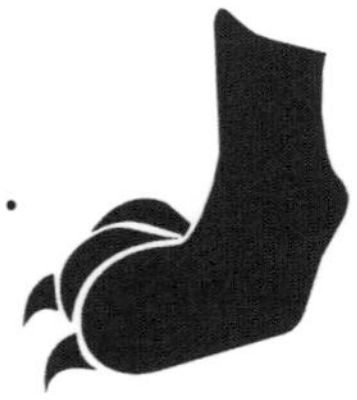 + len +  = ______________________________

2.  = ______________________________

3.  = ______________________________

4.  +  = ______________________________

5.  + 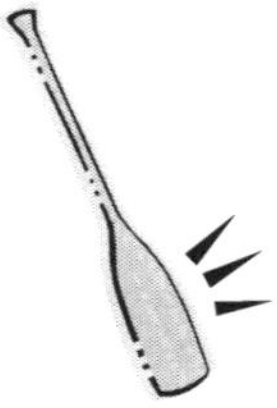 + M = ______________________________

Winning Delegates Through Caucuses & Primaries

Draw a line from each statement on the left to the correct match on the right.

1.	This state is the first to allow voters to express their preference among presidential candidates.	**California**
2.	This state holds the first presidential primary of the campaign season.	**closed primary**
3.	This is a vote in which only registered members of a certain political party can participate.	**Iowa**
4.	This is a meeting held by a political party to choose a candidate to support.	**New Hampshire**
5.	This state sends the most delegates to the Republican National Convention.	**caucus**

Lesson 34

Democratic and Republican Conventions

Complete this crossword puzzle.

Across

1. Who held their first national convention in 1832?
3. The 1968 Democratic Convention took place during a war in which country?
5. What is the name for a major speech (or address) at a convention?
7. Which city has hosted the most national conventions?

Down

2. What is the term for putting someone forward as a candidate at a convention?
4. A person who attends a convention to participate in the decision-making is called what?
6. Who held their first national convention in 1856?
8. What is the name for the document that describes the beliefs of a political party?

Amy, Jimmy, and Rosalynn Carter at the Democratic National Convention 1976

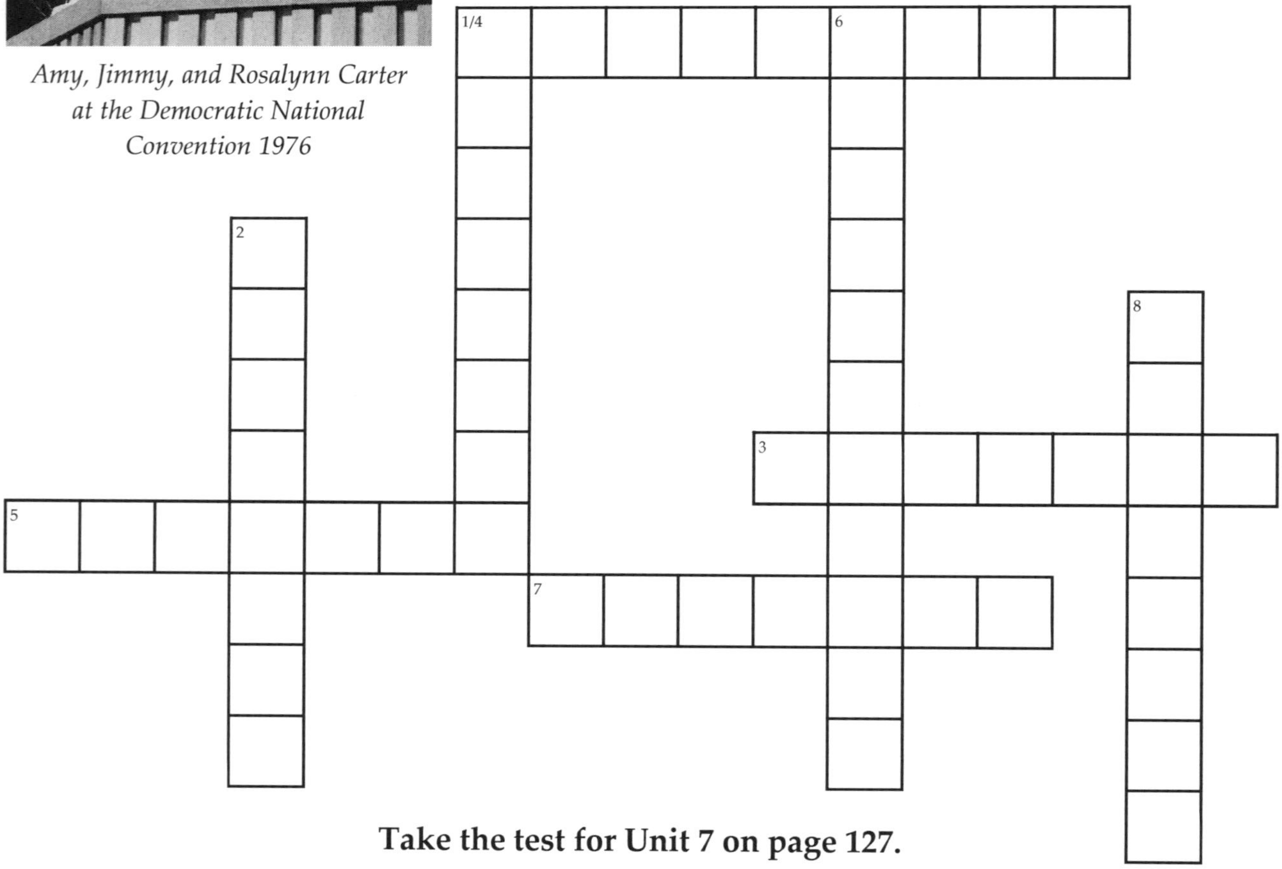

Take the test for Unit 7 on page 127.

Putting Together a Campaign

Use these words to fill in the blanks below. Be sure to put one letter in each blank.

family volunteers nominees voters
incumbents politicians artists mates

1. _ _ _ _ _ _ _ _ design campaign advertising.
2. _ _ _ _ _ _ _ _ _ _ _ stuff envelopes to mail to voters.
3. Campaign teams work to register _ _ _ _ _ _.
4. _ _ _ _ _ _ _ _ _ _ _ sometimes run Rose Garden campaigns.
5. _ _ _ _ _ _ _ _ _ appear in person and on television.
6. Each pair of running _ _ _ _ _ and their campaign workers join forces with their party to form a powerful campaign team.
7. _ _ _ _ _ _ members may work in the spotlight or behind the scenes to help their relative be elected.
8. Campaign teams schedule appearances by well-known _ _ _ _ _ _ _ _ _ _ _ who are willing to speak on behalf of a candidate.

Advertising Your Candidate

Fill in each blank with the word that completes the slogan or the name of the President who used it in his campaign.

"__________ with Dick" Nixon for President – *Richard Nixon*

It's ______________ Again in America – *Ronald Reagan*

A ______________ in Every Pot and a Car in Every Garage – *Herbert Hoover*

A Full ______________ Pail – *William McKinley*

I Like ________ – *Dwight D. Eisenhower*

A Leader for a ______________ – *Jimmy Carter*

A Time for ___________________ – *John F. Kennedy*

Keep ________ with Coolidge – *Calvin Coolidge*

The ____________ Are Too High for You to Stay at Home – *Lyndon B. Johnson*

Vote Yourself a ________ – *Abraham Lincoln*

Traveling the Campaign Trail

Imagine that you are a reporter following a presidential candidate on the campaign trail. On the map below, the dots represent cities. Using information in the paragraph below, draw lines between the dots to trace the route the candidate takes. You will not use all of the dots. If you need help identifying the states, look at the map on page 2 of this student workbook.

The candidate starts with a speech in Colorado. Then he has a fundraiser in California. Next is a meeting with business leaders in Texas. He goes to a debate in Georgia, attends another fundraiser in Ohio, and ends the week with a visit to our nation's capital, which lies along the border between Virginia and Maryland.

Puck *Magazine cartoon shows presidential candidate William Jennings Bryan traveling around the country giving speeches, September 16, 1896.*

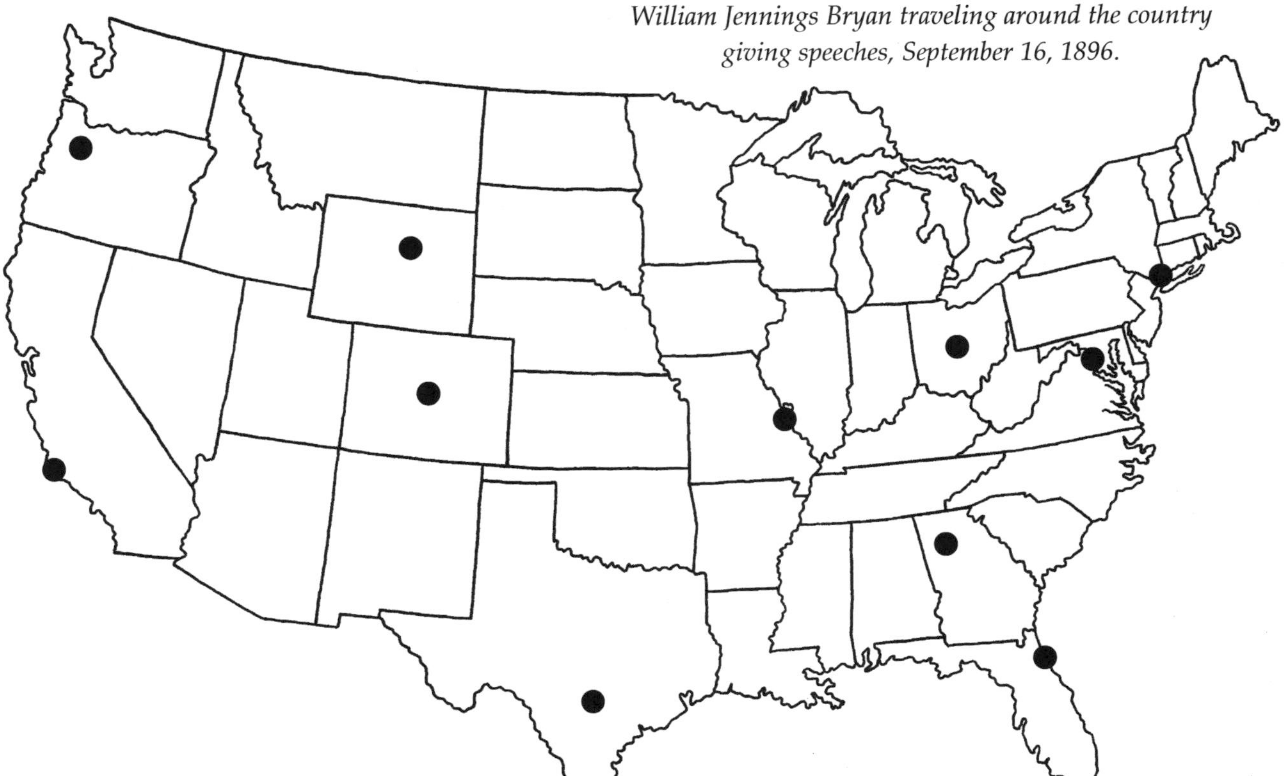

Lesson 39

The Presidential Debates

Lincoln-Douglas Debate

Hidden in the puzzle below are the names of five of the colleges, theaters, and performing arts centers that have hosted presidential debates. The names of seven Presidents who have participated in presidential debates are also hidden in the puzzle. Find the names of the Presidents and cross them out. Write the remaining letters in the spaces below.

RONALD GEORGE BILL
GEORGE BARACK
JOHN JIMMY GERALD

GEORGEBELMONTUNIVERSITYRONALD
BILLCENTRECOLLEGEJIMMYBARACK
GERALDUNIVERSITYOFMISSISSIPPI
GEORGEMAHAFFEYTHEATERJOHN
BUSHNELLPERFORMINGARTSCENTER

NASHVILLE, TENNESSEE - _ _ _ _ _ _ _ _   _ _ _ _ _ _ _ _ _ _ _ _

DANVILLE, KENTUCKY - _ _ _ _ _ _ _   _ _ _ _ _ _ _ _

OXFORD, MISSISSIPPI - _ _ _ _ _ _ _ _ _ _ _ _   _ _   _ _ _ _ _ _ _ _ _ _ _ _ _

ST. PETERSBURG, FLORIDA - _ _ _ _ _ _ _ _ _ _   _ _ _ _ _ _ _ _

HARTFORD, CONNECTICUT - _ _ _ _ _ _ _ _ _ _   _ _ _ _ _ _ _ _ _ _ _ _

_ _ _ _   _ _ _ _ _ _ _

Take the test for Unit 8 on page 128.

Getting Ready for Election Day

In the puzzle below, find these languages that are used on ballots in some locations.

BANGLADESHI	**CHINESE**	**CHOCTAW**
FILIPINO	**INUPIAT**	**JAPANESE**
KICKAPOO	**KOREAN**	**NAVAJO**
PUEBLO	**SPANISH**	**VIETNAMESE**

Q	J	Z	I	O	W	E	R	H	G	W	Y	U	B	F	D
W	A	X	U	K	Q	B	T	J	S	P	A	N	I	S	H
E	P	C	Y	J	A	A	Y	K	F	V	G	D	Y	E	R
R	A	V	I	E	T	N	A	M	E	S	E	F	U	N	F
T	N	V	T	G	S	G	U	L	D	X	W	I	Y	G	R
N	E	B	R	F	D	L	I	P	S	R	C	L	T	G	T
A	S	N	K	D	F	A	O	O	A	P	D	I	E	V	G
V	E	M	O	S	G	D	P	I	Q	U	G	P	W	X	U
A	D	L	R	A	H	E	L	U	W	E	D	I	E	C	B
J	F	K	E	Z	J	S	K	Y	E	B	B	N	Y	H	E
O	H	J	A	X	K	H	J	T	R	L	U	O	T	I	U
Y	G	I	N	U	P	I	A	T	T	O	E	G	V	N	N
U	H	F	Q	C	L	H	A	E	Y	U	Y	E	W	E	S
I	J	G	A	V	M	G	S	W	U	I	R	V	R	S	R
O	K	K	I	C	K	A	P	O	O	Y	T	U	R	E	W
P	L	D	S	B	N	D	C	H	O	C	T	A	W	T	R

Lesson 42

Going to the Polls on Election Day

Use the following words to fill in the blanks below:

precinct votes watchers registered
private box screen button treasures

1. A voter votes at the assigned polling place for his ____________.
2. Candidates may not enter polling places on Election Day, except to cast their own personal __________.
3. Candidates can send poll __________________ to the polls to make sure that an election is conducted fairly.
4. Poll workers check to see if a voter is _________________.
5. Today voters are guaranteed the right to vote in ____________.
6. When people use paper ballots, they drop them into a ballot _______.
7. Voters using Direct Recording Electronic voting machines touch a touch ______________ or push a _____________ to record their votes.
8. When a son receives his father's words and ________________ his commandments within him, that son will discern righteousness and justice and equity and every good course.

Farmers gather to vote in McIntosh County, North Dakota, 1940.

Finding Out Election Results

The pictures below show different ways that people have heard about election results over the years. Write the name of each technology below each picture.

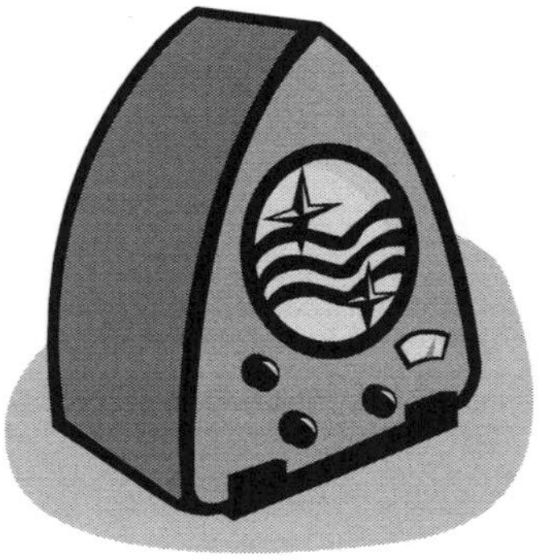

Lesson 44

The Electoral College and the Transition Team

Answer these questions based on the information in the lesson.

1. In the early 1800s, the group of people who cast the final votes for President and Vice President became known as the

   ________________________________.

2. The total number of electors from all fifty states plus the District of Columbia who vote in the Electoral College is _______.

3. The two states that allocate their electoral votes by congressional district are _________________ and

   _________________________.

4. A candidate must have _________ electoral votes to be elected President.

5. The agency of the Federal government that helps an incoming President and Vice President transition into their new jobs is the General ________________ Administration.

Electoral College cartoon shows Candidate William Jennings Bryan with Uncle Sam, Cover of Puck *Magazine, June 12, 1907.*

Take the test for Unit 9 on page 129.

Introducing the People of Washington, D.C.

Circle the correct answer beneath each question.

1. About how many people live in Washington, D.C.?

a. 60,000 b. 600,000 c. 6,000,000

2. Which hotel is known as the Hotel of Presidents?

a. Willard Hotel b. Peabody Hotel c. Anthony's Hotel

3. Someone who is employed to try to influence the votes of Senators and Congressmen is called what?

a. lunatic b. legalist c. lobbyist

4. Who cast the church bell for St. John's Episcopal Church?

a. Joseph Revere b. Betsy Ross c. Charles Ingalls

5. Which of these universities was founded to teach deaf and hearing impaired students?

a. Georgetown b. Gallaudet c. American

6. Which of these teams is **not** a professional sports team based in Washington, D.C.?

a. Redskins b. Mystics c. Vikings

Washington, D.C. Cherry Blossoms

Lesson 47

Becoming the Capital City

Complete this Capital City timeline by filling in the blanks below.

1783	An angry mob in Philadelphia drove ______________ away from the city.
1787	The Constitution authorized the creation of a District to become the _______ of the Government.
1790	Congress decided that the capital of the United States would be located along the ______________ River.
1792	The cornerstone was laid for the _________________ Mansion, now known as the White House.
1793	The ________________ was laid for the Capitol.
November 1, 1800	President ____________________ moved into the Executive Mansion.
November 17, 1800	Congress held its first sessions in the ___________________.
1803	Thomas Jefferson hired Benjamin Henry ______________ to continue work on the Capitol.

From Mud Streets to Grand Avenues

Complete this crossword puzzle.

Across

1. This President fled Washington D.C., during the War of 1812.
3. The plan to build this system was abandoned after railroads became important.
5. People in this state asked Congress to return the land they had ceded to build Washington, D.C.
7. During the Civil War, many troops were stationed in Washington, D.C., to protect it against this army.

Down

2. This architect was one of the first city councilmen in Washington, D.C.
4. A National Cemetery with the Tomb of the Unknowns is located in this Virginia city.
6. This sculptor worked with architects in the 20th century to make Washington, D.C., more beautiful.
8. The city of Washington, D.C., is led by this elected official.

Timeline of D.C. National Park Sites

In the puzzle below are the names of several national park sites, plus six careers pursued by National Park Service employees. Cross out the names of these parks and then you will be able to read the careers. Write the names of the careers in the blanks below.

LINCOLN MEMORIAL YOSEMITE
YELLOWSTONE GRAND CANYON
SMOKY MOUNTIANS
MESA VERDE
JEFFERSON MEMORIAL

YOSEMITEHYDROLOGISTYELLOWSTONE
GEOLOGISTSMOKYMOUNTAINSFORESTRYTECHNICIAN
LINCOLNMEMORIALPARKRANGER
GRANDCANYONCARPENTER
JEFFERSONMEMORIALBOTANISTMESAVERDE

_ _ _ _ _ _ _ _ _ _ _ _ _

_ _ _ _ _ _ _ _ _ _ _

_ _ _ _ _ _ _ _ _ _   _ _ _ _ _ _ _ _ _ _ _ _

_ _ _ _   _ _ _ _ _ _ _

_ _ _ _ _ _ _ _ _ _ _

_ _ _ _ _ _ _ _ _ _

Take the test for Unit 10 on page 130.

Responsibilities of the President

Write each word from the list on the correct blank to complete each sentence.

Ambassadors	**pardons**	**Cabinet**
State of the Union	**executive**	**head of state**
Commander in Chief	**Chief of Staff**	**judges**

1. The President leads the ________________ branch.
2. The heads of Federal departments who meet with and advise the President are called the ______________.
3. The person who works for the President in overseeing work at the White House is called the _________________________.
4. As the highest-ranking representative of our government in relating to foreign governments, the President is the _________________________.
5. The President is also called the ____________________________ because he is in charge of all U.S. military forces.
6. The President appoints ____________________ to represent the United States in foreign countries.
7. The President appoints ___________ to serve in Federal courts.
8. The President can issue _____________ to people who have been convicted of crimes against the United States.
9. The President's annual speech to Congress is called the __________________________________.

Lesson 52

The Leadership Role of the President

Read this paragraph and put each word in ALL CAPS in its correct location in the puzzle below.

The President makes personal APPEARANCES and gives SPEECHES around the country. He receives visits from HEADS OF STATE and travels to other countries. At the White House, the President hosts STATE DINNERS and presents AWARDS to especially brave soldiers and prominent citizens. He also answers questions from reporters at PRESS CONFERENCES. For his safety, the President travels in an armored LIMOUSINE, a Marine helicopter, and a custom airplane known as AIR FORCE ONE. A sitting President is considered the LEADER of his political party. President Roosevelt said that he had a BULLY PULPIT from which to share his views.

President George W. Bush

The President's Day

President and Mrs. Bush board Air Force One.

Draw a line from each time on the left to the matching activity on the right that occupied President George H. W. Bush's time on November 30, 1989.

1. **5:45 a.m.** •	• talked with his son Jeb Bush
2. **8:00 a.m.** •	• headed for Malta aboard Air Force One
3. **9:41 a.m.** •	• received intelligence briefing
4. **10:58 a.m.** •	• talked with his mother
5. **12:05 p.m.** •	• had breakfast with the First Lady
6. **1:16 p.m.** •	• made a statement in the Rose Garden
7. **5:56 p.m.** •	• spoke by phone with the President of France
8. **6:54 p.m.** •	• had lunch with the Vice President

Lesson 54

The President's Cabinet

The President's Cabinet has many members, including the Secretaries of:

HOMELAND SECURITY   STATE   DEFENSE   LABOR   INTERIOR

Find each of those words in this puzzle. Each of the rebus puzzles below also represent one of those departments. Write the correct department beside each rebus.

U	D	E	F	E	N	S	E	A	U	S	A	U	S	T	A	T	E	A	U
S	U	H	O	M	E	L	A	N	D	S	E	C	U	R	I	T	Y	S	S
A	L	A	B	O	R	U	S	A	U	I	N	T	E	R	I	O	R	U	A

1.  + 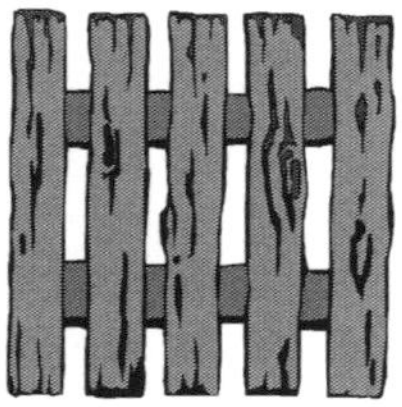 = ______________________

2. 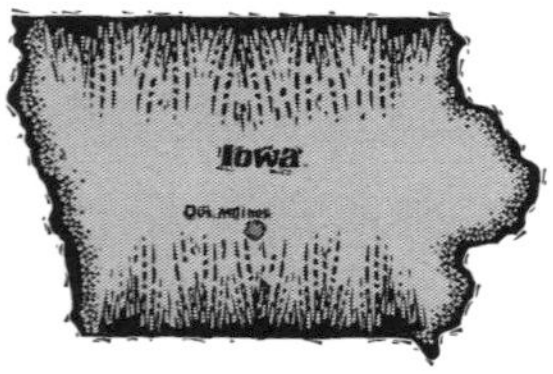

= ______________________

3. N +  **+ E +**  = ______________________

4.  +  **C +** 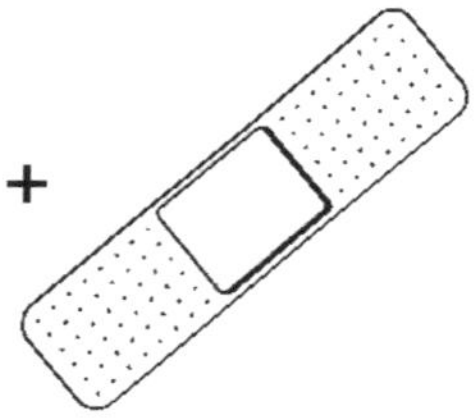 **+ I +** 

= ____

5.  +  = ______________________

Take the test for Unit 11 on page 131.

The Role of the First Lady

Write each first name beside the matching last name of these First Ladies.

Bess Betty Dolley Hillary Jacqueline

Lady Bird Laura Michelle Nancy Rosalynn

______________________ **Johnson**

______________________ **Ford**

______________________ **Obama**

______________________ **Carter**

______________________ **Clinton**

______________________ **Madison**

______________________ **Kennedy**

______________________ **Truman**

______________________ **Bush**

______________________ **Reagan**

While serving as Secretary of State, former First Lady Hillary Clinton meets with Hungarian Prime Minister Viktor Orban, June 2011.

Lesson 57

The White House

Follow these directions about rooms and features in the White House. The information is found on page 301 in the text.

1. Draw a flame below the number of fireplaces.
2. Draw an arrow above the number of doors.
3. Draw a triangle around the number of elevators.
4. Draw a circle around the number of bathrooms.
5. Draw a plus sign above the number of windows.
6. Draw a square around the number of rooms.
7. Draw a shoe above the number of staircases.

8

35

132

412

147

28

3

The White House Residence Staff

Design an invitation to an event at the White House. It could be a dinner honoring a special guest, an award ceremony, a birthday or Christmas party, or something else.

Lesson 59

Going Home to Monticello

Use these words to fill in the blanks below.

France **eight** **Indian artifacts**
models **polygraph** **maps**
Texas **Gettysburg**
little mountain **art** **Independence**

Monticello

1. The word "monticello" means ______________________________ in Italian.

2. Thomas Jefferson's role as Ambassador to ______________ influenced his design of Monticello.

3. Artifacts in the Entrance Hall of Monticello include ____________, ____, ______________, and ________________.

4. Jefferson used a ________________________ to make copies of his letters.

5. The North Octagonal Room has __________________ sides.

6. President Truman and his wife Bess returned to their home in ________________________________, Missouri.

7. President Eisenhower and his wife Mamie moved near the ______________________ Battlefield.

8. All three Presidents from ________________ returned there after serving as President.

Take the test for Unit 12 on page 132.

The United States Capitol

The U.S. Capitol features numerous paintings and sculptures that illustrate events in American history. Design an art work that represents an event in American history.

Lesson 62

Organization of the U.S. Congress

Solve these math problems.

1. 100 Senators + 435 Representatives = __________ elected members of Congress

2. If a Congressman is 44 years old, and he has been a U.S. citizen for seven years, how old was he when he became a citizen? _________

3. If 34 U.S. Senators seats are up for election in a certain year, how many Senate seats are not up for election? _________

4. If there are 100 U.S. Senators and their average age is 60, how many combined years have they lived? _________

5. If one-tenth of Senators are in favor of a certain bill, how many Senators is that? _________

6. If a Senator is elected in 2012, when would his next election be? _________

7. If a Representative is elected in 2014, when would his next election be? _________

Senator Rand Paul

How the U.S. Congress Works

Read these statements and put each word in ALL CAPS in its correct location in the puzzle below.

The U.S. Congress is divided into a SENATE and a House of REPRESENTATIVES. Senators and Representatives are assigned to COMMITTEES to study particular pieces of legislation. *The Congressional RECORD* is a journal of what happens in Congress.

The Senate has many TRADITIONS such as the candy desk. In addition to voting on bills, the Senate provides advice and CONSENT to the President on nominations and treaties.

Marker for the location of Lincoln's desk in National Statuary Hall in the Capitol.

Each Senator and Congressman receives a SALARY plus additional money to pay for staff and offices. If they are running for re-election, they spend some time working on their CAMPAIGNS.

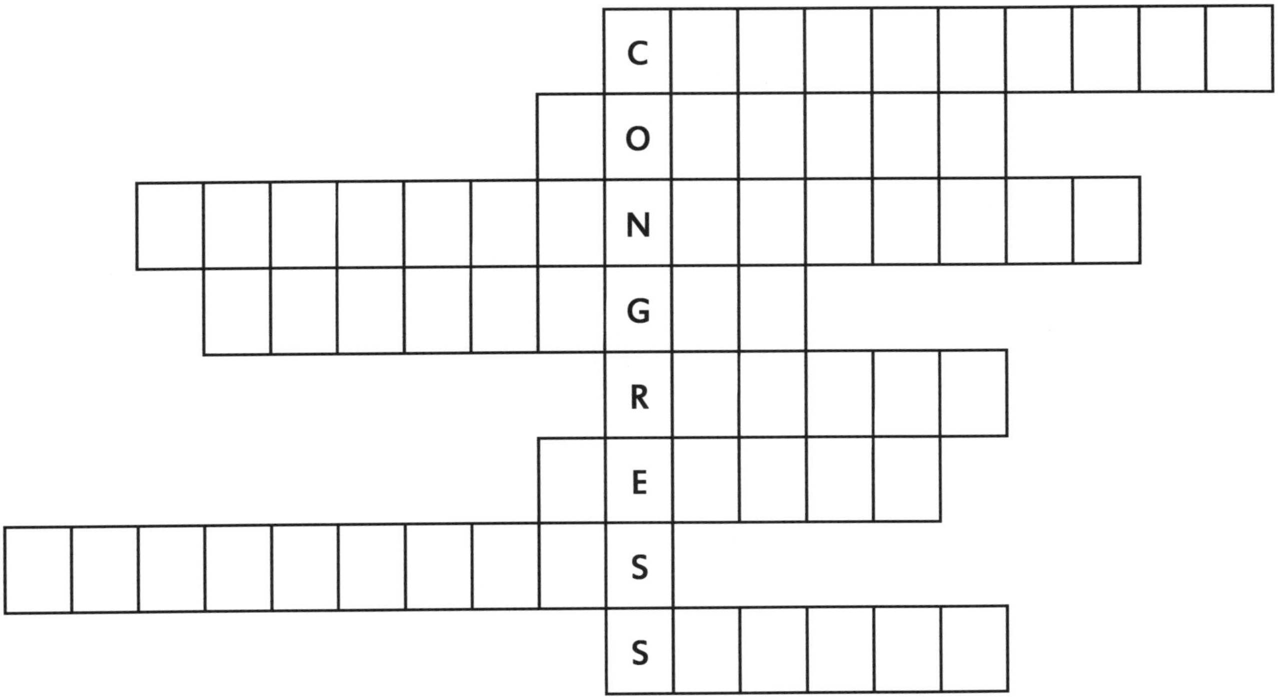

Lesson 64

How a Bill Becomes Law

Use these words to fill in the blanks below:

committee **full** **President**
conference **Clerk**
bill **Speaker** **debate**
revised **amendment**

1	Rep. Throckmorton's staff writes the ___________.
2	The House _____________ assigns the bill a number.
3	The ____________ of the House assigns the bill to a committee.
4	The House committee votes to recommend the bill to the _______ House of Representatives.
5	After ___________ in the House, the bill is approved.
6	The bill is assigned to a Senate _________________, which holds hearings and decides to recommend the bill.
7	The Senate approves the bill with an ______________________.
8	A ________________ committee approves a compromise version.
9	The _____________ bill passes both the House and Senate again.
10	The bill goes to the _________________ for his final decision.

Take the test for Unit 13 on page 133.

The Congressional Staff

Write the letter in front of each job in the blank beside the description of what that staff member does.

A. Chief of Staff

B. Director of Communications

C. Legislative Director

D. Legislative Counsel

E. Legislative Assistant

F. Caseworker

G. Receptionist

H. Scheduler

Seal on the Exterior of the Rayburn House Office Building

_____ Meets with lobbyists and voters

_____ Keeps up with bills and provides information on them

_____ Makes appointments and travel arrangements

_____ Oversees other staff and advises the member of Congress

_____ Helps citizens deal with Federal agencies

_____ Provides legal advice

_____ Manages interaction with the media

_____ Answers the phone and greets visitors

Working on Capitol Hill

Capitol Woodcrafter

Representatives and Senators get most of the attention, but many other people do important jobs that help Congress do its work. In the puzzle below, find these jobs that people perform on Capitol Hill.

ACCOUNTANT	**ARCHITECT**	**CONSERVATOR**
ECONOMIST	**ELECTRICIAN**	**ENGINEER**
GROUNDSKEEPER	**GUIDE**	**PAINTER**
PLASTERER	**POLICE OFFICER**	**PRINTER**

E	P	Q	P	L	A	S	T	E	R	E	R	G	H	O	J
W	A	W	N	M	C	W	M	L	C	Q	W	R	G	I	E
T	I	E	B	L	C	R	N	K	Z	Y	R	O	F	U	L
U	N	R	V	E	O	T	B	J	C	U	G	U	I	D	E
G	T	T	C	N	U	Y	V	H	O	I	S	N	D	Y	C
D	E	Y	X	G	N	U	C	G	N	O	Z	D	S	T	T
A	R	C	H	I	T	E	C	T	S	K	X	S	A	R	R
V	E	I	Z	N	A	I	X	F	E	J	C	K	Q	E	I
P	R	U	A	E	N	O	Z	D	R	H	S	E	T	W	C
R	T	O	S	E	T	P	A	S	V	G	Q	E	E	C	I
I	U	P	D	R	S	L	S	A	A	F	W	P	U	R	A
N	E	C	O	N	O	M	I	S	T	D	T	E	H	W	N
T	B	L	F	K	D	K	D	Q	O	S	R	R	G	V	U
E	S	K	G	J	F	J	F	W	R	A	E	S	F	R	I
R	P	O	L	I	C	E	O	F	F	I	C	E	R	T	O
X	Z	J	H	H	G	H	G	E	R	T	Y	U	I	O	P

The Office of Vice President

Circle the correct answer beneath each question.

1. The Constitution says that the Vice President is president of what?

a. the Senate　　b. the House　　c. the Supreme Court

2. How many times has a Vice President become President after the President died?

a. three　　b. eight　　c. twelve

3. What is the abbreviation for the daily top secret meeting in the Oval Office?

a. PBJ　　b. POD　　c. PDB

4. What is the name for the Vice President's office in the Eisenhower Executive Office Building?

a. Confrontational　　b. Ceremonial　　c. Confidential

5. Which Vice President signed the Nineteenth Amendment?

a. Thomas Marshall　　b. Dan Quayle　　c. Hubert Humphrey

6. Who became President after the death of Franklin Roosevelt in 1945?

a. Mike Pence　　b. Al Gore　　c. Harry Truman

7. What is the address of the Vice President's house?

a. 1776 Constitution Avenue

b. Number One Observatory Circle

c. Number Two Pennsylvania Avenue

Vice President Joe Biden, 2012

Lesson 69

The Library of Congress

Use these words to fill in the blanks to complete the timeline.

Congress John Adams fire Highsmith
James Madison smallest Thomas Jefferson

1800 ____________ set aside $5,000 to start a book collection.

1851 A __________ destroyed 35,000 books in the library.

1897 The ______________ ________________ Building opened.

1939 The ____________ _____________ Building opened.

1980 The __________ _______________ Building opened.

1985 The ___________________ book in the Library of Congress was published.

2010 Carol ________________ began a project to take photographs of America in the 21st Century.

Take the test for Unit 14 on page 134.

America and the World

In the puzzle below, find these words relating to America's relationship with other countries of the world.

OFFICIAL	**ALLY**
FOREIGN	**DIPLOMACY**
UNITED	**NATIONS**
SECURITY	**COUNCIL**
PEACE	**CONSULATE**
COUNTRY	**AMBASSADORS**
CONSULS	**RECOGNITION**
HOST	**GOVERNMENTS**

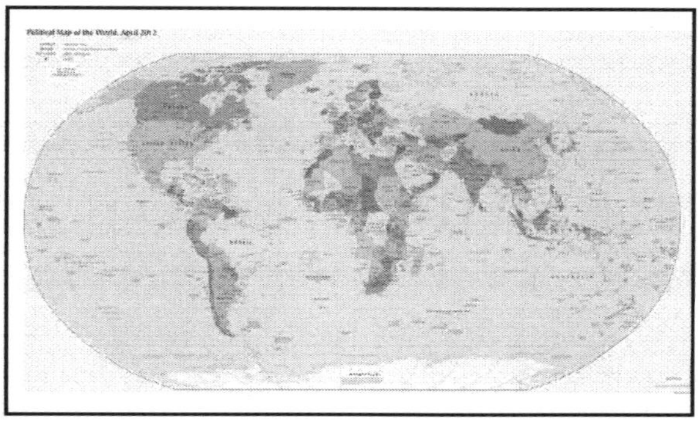

G	O	V	E	R	N	M	E	N	T	S	A	C	O	U	N	C	I	L	E
F	O	R	G	O	D	S	O	L	O	V	E	O	D	N	T	H	E	A	V
S	E	C	U	R	I	T	Y	G	A	V	E	N	A	I	B	U	T	A	E
W	O	R	L	D	L	O	V	E	D	H	E	S	A	T	H	A	V	E	R
T	H	A	T	A	A	L	L	Y	H	I	S	U	A	E	A	A	A	E	L
F	O	N	L	Y	S	O	N	T	H	A	T	L	A	D	I	N	M	T	A
O	P	E	R	I	S	H	A	D	A	A	A	A	N	O	T	A	B	E	S
R	E	C	O	G	N	I	T	I	O	N	A	T	A	A	A	A	A	R	T
E	A	O	A	A	A	A	A	P	A	A	A	E	A	P	A	A	S	N	I
I	A	N	A	A	T	A	A	L	L	I	F	E	A	E	A	A	S	A	N
G	A	S	A	A	I	A	A	O	F	F	I	C	I	A	L	A	A	K	G
N	A	U	A	A	O	A	A	M	S	H	A	L	L	C	A	A	D	A	A
A	A	L	A	A	N	A	A	A	A	A	A	A	A	E	A	A	O	A	A
H	O	S	T	A	S	A	A	C	H	I	M	A	A	A	A	A	R	A	A
W	H	O	E	V	E	R	A	Y	B	E	L	I	E	V	E	S	S	A	A
B	E	G	O	T	T	E	N	A	A	A	C	O	U	N	T	R	Y	A	A

Lesson 72

Presidential Visits Around the World

The lines on the map below point to countries visited for the first time by a certain President in a certain year. Using this list, write the name of the correct country on each blank.

Australia Botswana Canada China Colombia
Cuba France Hungary Liberia Pakistan

2. ____________________
(Bush, 1989)

1. ____________________
(Wilson, 1919)

5. ____________________
(Harding, 1923)

3. ____________________
(Eisenhower, 1959)

4. ____________________
(Nixon, 1972)

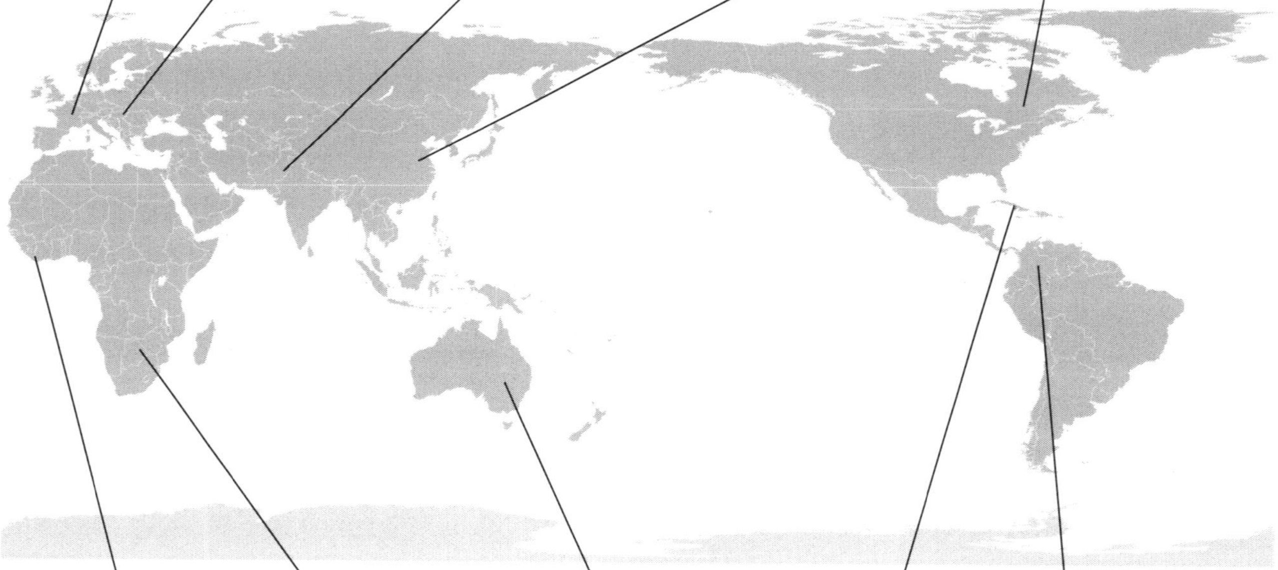

8. ____________________
(Johnson, 1966)

7. ____________________
(Clinton, 1998)

9. ____________________
(Coolidge, 1928)

6. ____________________
(F. Roosevelt, 1943)

10. ____________________
(Kennedy, 1961)

The Work of an Ambassador

Draw a line from the word on the left to the statement on the right that is missing that word.

PROTOCOL •	• 1. Ambassadors are appointed by the President and confirmed by the ___________________.
OATH •	• 2. The executive department that helps the President with diplomatic relations is the Department of ______________.
SENATE •	• 3. Rights and privileges given to Ambassadors in the past have developed into accepted ways of doing things called ____________.
CHRIST •	• 4. An Ambassador-at-____________ represents the U.S. in several countries in a certain region of the world.
STATE •	• 5. Like many other government officials, an Ambassador takes an _______ of office.
ENVOYS •	• 6. Christians are ambassadors for _______________.
LARGE •	• 7. Heads of state use ______________ to carry out specific missions for a given length of time.

Lesson 74

A Drive Down Embassy Row

The countries represented by these flags have embassies in Washington, D.C. Unscramble the name of each of these countries.

JAPAN CANADA EGYPT INDIA NORWAY UNITED KINGDOM
TURKEY ESTONIA SPAIN MEXICO CHILE SOUTH AFRICA

AAANCD

____

TNUDEI KGMNIOD

____

KYUTER

____

GPYET

____

NIIAD

____

IEOXMC

____

IECLH

____

RANWYO

____

PNIAS

____

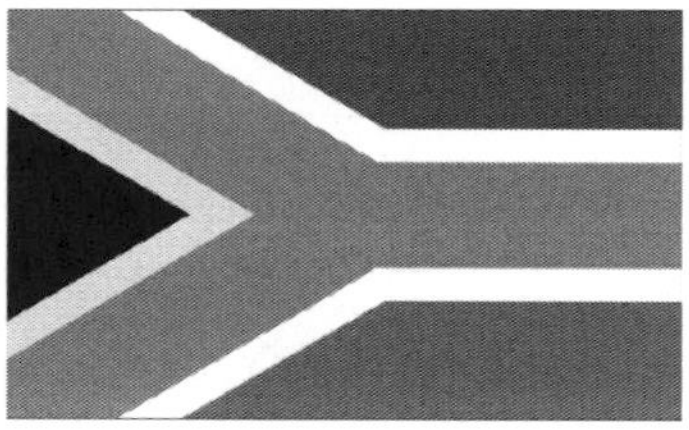

OSHTU RFAACI

____

APNAJ

____

TENAOSI

____

Take the test for Unit 15 on page 135.

The United States Military I

Find the last name of each President who served in the military in the puzzle below.

Arthur
Buchanan
Bush
Bush
Carter
Eisenhower
Fillmore
Ford
Garfield
Grant
Harrison
Harrison
Hayes
Jackson
Jefferson
Johnson
Johnson
Kennedy
Lincoln
Madison
McKinley
Monroe
Nixon
Pierce
Polk
Reagan
Roosevelt
Taylor
Truman
Tyler
Washington

Major General Zachary Taylor

E	H	A	R	R	I	S	O	N	E	B	U	C	H	A	N	A	N	B	A	W	E	R	A
D	G	U	E	I	O	P	L	K	T	A	D	C	A	V	X	Z	B	U	S	H	D	E	C
K	V	Y	A	A	M	C	K	I	N	L	E	Y	R	F	C	X	Z	S	S	D	C	I	V
E	E	T	G	R	R	S	X	A	F	P	I	E	R	C	E	Q	W	H	A	Y	E	S	S
N	W	F	A	T	X	C	V	B	I	Z	W	N	I	X	O	N	E	R	T	J	G	E	D
N	Q	C	N	H	F	E	F	E	L	A	A	S	S	R	V	F	C	H	Y	O	F	N	M
E	G	V	T	U	S	S	O	F	L	S	S	W	O	F	M	E	X	B	T	H	D	H	O
D	A	C	A	R	T	E	R	C	M	D	H	E	N	V	A	R	J	O	H	N	S	O	N
Y	R	Q	Y	E	R	T	D	S	O	F	I	D	C	W	D	T	A	T	B	S	X	W	R
T	F	W	L	Q	E	G	C	G	R	A	N	T	X	Y	I	Y	C	R	V	O	C	E	O
U	I	E	O	S	F	F	V	X	E	C	G	Y	P	I	S	U	K	E	F	N	V	R	E
J	E	T	R	U	M	A	N	C	D	X	T	L	O	R	O	O	S	E	V	E	L	T	F
H	L	F	V	S	D	F	G	V	W	S	O	E	L	I	N	C	O	L	N	T	E	W	D
F	D	D	J	E	F	F	E	R	S	O	N	R	K	X	Z	N	N	F	E	R	D	S	A

Lesson 77

The United States Military II

The four branches of the U.S. military are the Army, Navy, Air Force, and Marines. Write the name of each branch under the photo that illustrates the primary area of responsibility for that branch.

Do you have any family members who have served in the military? Write their names below. Ask your parent if you are not sure.

Name	Relation to You	Branch of Military

Four Years at West Point

Answer these questions about West Point.

1. Whom did General Washington instruct to design a fortress at West Point in 1778? Draw a box around his name.

2. Which President signed the legislation creating the U.S. Military Academy at West Point? Draw a flag next to his name.

3. What general emphasized physical fitness as Superintendent of West Point after World War I? Draw a man running next to his name.

4. What are the nicknames for the Cadets during each year of training at West Point? Write the number 1 next to the first year student nickname, 2 next to the second year nickname, 3 next to the third, and 4 next to the fourth.

Dwight D. Eisenhower

Thaddeus Kosciuszko

Benedict Arnold

plebes

Ulysses S. Grant

Douglas MacArthur

mules

Nathanael Greene

firsties

yearlings

Thomas Jefferson

George Washington

cows

puppies

Cadet Chapel at West Point

Lesson 79

Three Days of Marine Basic Training

Complete this maze going from Start to Finish. Rescue the wounded soldiers by taking a path that leads you past each figure in the maze.

Take the test for Unit 16 on page 136.

In the State Capital

Unscramble the names of the state government departments below. This list of department names will help you. You will not use all of them.

Agriculture	Corrections
Education	Health
Human Services	Public Safety
Revenue	Social Services
Tourism	Transportation
Tribal Relations	Veterans Affairs

The South Dakota Plumbing Commission is part of the state Department of Labor and Regulation. This is its office in the capital city of Pierre.

ETHLHA ______________________________

NEREEUV ______________________________

RRCAUGLTIUE ______________________________

MNUHA VECRSISE ______________________________

EVTRESAN FFASIAR ______________________________

DAUECITNO ______________________________

At the State Capitol

Draw a line from each photo of a state capitol to the matching state. The name of the capital city is shown with each photo. Each of the matches is mentioned in either Lesson 81 or 82.

Hawaii

Nevada

Wisconsin

Iowa

Montana

In the Governor's Office

Governors have many activities to keep them busy. Look at the captions under the pictures in this lesson. Fill in the blanks below by writing the name of the state each Governor is from who is pictured doing that activity.

Washington Governor Chris Gregoire (left) and Oregon Governor John Kitzhaber spoke at a news conference in 2011 about improving transportation across the Columbia River between the two states.

1) Visiting China on a trade mission:

____

2) Congratulating a Senator for fifty years of service:

____

3) Speaking at the National Elk Refuge Centennial Ceremony:

____

4) Visiting a General in Afghanistan:

______________________ and ______________________

5) Attending a BBQ:

____

Lesson 84

Around the State

Look at a real license plate and design two new license plates. One of them should represent something about your state such as a natural feature or a tourist attraction. The other should represent a certain organization or idea that is important to a large number of people in your state (such as a sports team, a university, or being pro-life). Be sure to include the name of your state somewhere on both plates.

Take the test for Unit 17 on page 137.

At the County Courthouse

Read each statement. Draw an X over the word below each statement that does not belong.

1) Names for an area of U.S. government smaller than a state.

county parish shire

2) Vehicles that citizens can drive on Mackinac Island.

SUV bicycle horse-drawn wagon

3) Parts of the America's Center Convention Complex in St. Louis.

Six Flags Ferrara Theatre Edward Jones Dome

4) Names for county government officials.

commissioner supervisor dictator

5) Jobs performed by a county treasurer.

collecting taxes printing money paying bills

Pima County Courthouse, Tuscon, AZ

Lesson 87

Around City Hall

Read these statements and put each word in ALL CAPS in its correct location in the puzzle below.

The process of starting a new town is called INCORPORATION. A new city receives a CHARTER from the state government giving the people certain rights and responsibilities.

Most cities have a city COUNCIL that makes decisions about how to run the city. Some cities hire a manager who oversees the daily work, while other cities elect a MAYOR to do that job. A few cities are run by a COMMISSION.

A city provides SERVICES such as police protection and street MAINTENANCE. It must collect TAXES to pay for these services. CITY HALL is often the place where citizens can find government offices.

City Council Meeting in Columbia, MO

Working Together for a Stop Sign

Draw a picture of a stop sign and its surroundings. It could be a real stop sign close to your house or an imaginary one.

Hometown Celebrations

Think about a festival that your community could host. Look at the list of questions at the beginning of lesson 89 for ideas about choosing a theme. Fill in the blanks below with your ideas.

Name of Your Festival: ______________________________

Why You Picked This Theme: ______________________________

____

____

____

Time of Year to Hold It: ______________________________

Activities You Would Like to Have:

____

____

____

____

Person Who Could Be Master of Ceremonies (either someone who lives in your community or a famous person):

____

Take the test for Unit 18 on page 138.

Lesson 91

The Bureau of Indian Affairs

Read these statements and put each word in ALL CAPS in its correct location in the puzzle below.

The FEDERAL Bureau of Indian Affairs is involved with American INDIANS and ALASKA Natives.

These men have served as leaders in U.S. relations with Native Americans: Benjamin FRANKLIN, John C. CALHOUN, Ely S. PARKER, and Robert L. BENNETT.

One of the Native Americans visiting WASHINGTON, D.C., in 1863 was wearing a JEFFERSON PEACE MEDAL.

In 1923 PUEBLO leaders visiting Washington, D.C., brought a CANE given to them by President Abraham LINCOLN.

Photos in Lesson 91 include people of the SIOUX, IROQUOIS, and CHEYENNE TRIBES and the TULALIP Reservation.

Among the tribes listed in the chart on page 595 are the MENOMINEE and ONEIDA.

Lesson 92

Native American Tribes and Reservations

Use the instructions below to color a pattern on this blanket design.

Color the state with the lowest number of Native Americans in 2010 red.
Color the state with the highest number of Native Americans in 2010 green.
Native tribes continue to apply to the Federal government for ___________. Color it green.
Color the capital city of the Navajo Nation red.
Color the 250 people who help Navajo courts green.
Color the building completed by the Works Progress Administration in 1935 red.
Color the shape of the building red.
Color the Navajo people who helped create a secret code during World War II green.
Color another word for Navajo communities red.
Navajoland covers land in three states. Color each of these states red.
Color each square with a large letter in it green.

N		Vermont		peacemakers	
	A		octagonal		Code Talkers
Navajo Council Chambers		V		Arizona	
	chapters		A		Utah
California		Window Rock		J	
	recognition		New Mexico		O

Native Americans and the States

In the puzzle below, find the fifteen states with more than 100,000 Native Americans. Also find the names of the Native Americans who are honored with statues in Statuary Hall.

ALASKA
ARIZONA
CALIFORNIA
COLORADO
FLORIDA
ILLINOIS
MICHIGAN
MINNESOTA
NEW MEXICO
NEW YORK
NORTH CAROLINA
OKLAHOMA
OREGON
TEXAS
WASHINGTON
PO'PAY
SEQUOYAH
SAKAKAWEA
WASHAKIE
SARAH WINNEMUCCA
WILL ROGERS

S	A	K	A	K	A	W	E	A	N	E	W	M	E	X	I	C	O	C	O	D	E	T	A	L
U	N	C	L	E	S	A	M	A	M	E	R	I	C	A	T	H	E	B	E	A	U	T	I	F
A	W	L	M	N	O	W	P	Q	R	S	T	U	V	W	W	O	X	Y	Z	A	B	F	K	U
S	A	R	A	H	W	I	N	N	E	M	U	C	C	A	C	K	D	E	F	G	H	L	E	L
A	S	J	K	L	M	L	N	O	P	Q	R	S	T	S	A	L	A	S	K	A	U	O	R	I
B	H	V	W	X	Y	L	Z	A	B	C	D	E	F	H	G	A	H	I	J	R	K	R	L	C
C	I	M	N	O	O	R	E	G	O	N	P	O'	P	A	Y	H	T	I	U	I	V	I	W	O
D	N	N	E	W	Y	O	R	K	X	Y	R	T	Y	K	Y	O	D	L	E	Z	F	D	G	L
E	G	H	I	F	E	G	A	B	C	D	W	A	G	I	Y	M	E	L	F	O	G	A	H	O
F	T	E	X	A	S	E	O	P	Q	R	S	T	U	E	V	A	W	I	X	N	Y	Z	I	R
G	O	A	B	C	D	R	A	B	C	D	E	F	G	A	H	I	J	N	K	A	L	M	J	A
H	N	G	H	I	J	S	E	Q	U	O	Y	A	H	W	N	O	P	O	Q	R	S	T	K	D
I	K	L	M	N	O	P	Q	R	S	T	U	V	W	X	Y	Z	A	I	U	V	W	X	L	O
N	O	R	T	H	C	A	R	O	L	I	N	A	Y	Z	A	B	C	S	D	E	F	G	M	H
N	A	V	A	J	O	C	O	D	E	T	A	L	M	I	N	N	E	S	O	T	A	E	E	A
J	K	C	A	L	I	F	O	R	N	I	A	M	I	C	H	I	G	A	N	I	J	K	N	L

Lesson 94

Native American Heritage Month

Native Americans use objects that have been traditional parts of various tribal cultures to celebrate Native American Heritage Month. Some are pictured below. To the left of each picture is a number. Unscramble the words beside the matching numbers to identify some of these objects that they use:

SPEAR PAINT FEATHERS MITTENS SHELLS BOOTS DRUM BOW & ARROW SHIELD

7

5

3

4

1. LSSLEH ______________
2. OSTBO ______________
3. OWB & RAWOR ____________________
4. TIMNEST ______________
5. NPITA ______________
6. EHSIDL ______________
7. APSRE ______________
8. UDMR ______________
9. ERTEFASH ______________

9

1

8

6

2

Take the test for Unit 19 on page 139.

Helping Our Country Be Safe

An acronym is used to abbreviate a long name or phrase. For example, USA is an acronym for United States of America. Many government agencies are commonly referred to by acronyms. Circle the acronyms of the agencies mentioned in this lesson.

TVA

CBP

FEMA

PBS

HHS

FDA

USCIS

ICE

CIA

FBI

TSA

HSI

NPR

Lesson 97

The Secret Service

Complete this crossword puzzle.

Across

1. This President authorized the formation of the Secret Service.
3. This President voluntarily gave up Secret Service protection.
5. The Secret Service provided protection for the wife and children of this President after he was assassinated.
7. Stealing personal information from someone and pretending to be that person is called this kind of theft.

Down

2. This is the term for printing fake money.
4. This is another name for paper money.
6. The Secret Service provides protection for about 170 of these in Washington, D.C.

This Secret Service agent is helping to protect the motorcade of the Prime Minister of India during a visit to Washington, D.C., in 2009.

Protecting America's Borders

Find America's borders. Trace the border (shown by a dotted line) between Canada and the U.S. in red. Trace the border between the U.S. and Mexico (also a dotted line) in green. Trace the parts of the United States that touch an ocean or a gulf in blue. Draw a brown line between Russia and Alaska and between the U.S. and Cuba.

Lesson 99

When an Immigrant Becomes a Citizen

Read these statements and put each word in ALL CAPS in its correct location in the puzzle below.

About 700,000 immigrants become CITIZENS of the United States every year. They come from dozens of countries, including MEXICO, INDIA, the PHILIPPINES, CHINA, and VIETNAM. Many of these immigrants become citizens while living in CALIFORNIA, New York, Florida, Texas, or New Jersey.

To become a U.S. citizen, an immigrant must be able to read, write, and speak basic English; show a basic understanding of U.S. history and GOVERNMENT; and take the Oath of Allegiance to the CONSTITUTION.

Naturalization Ceremony at the Grand Canyon, 2010

Take the test for Unit 20 on page 140.

Call 9-1-1

Draw a line between the descriptions on the left and the matching person or place on the right.

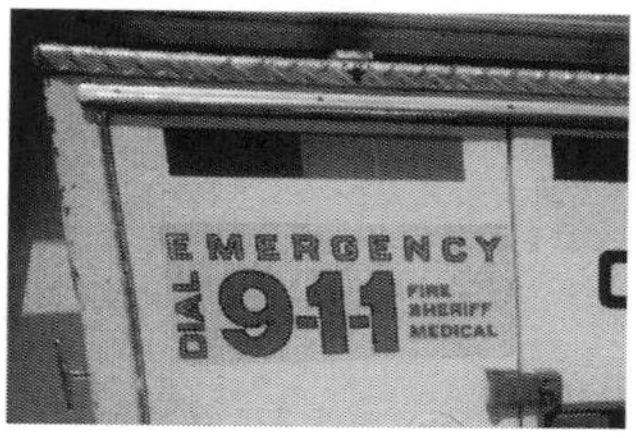

Emergency Vehicle in California

Made the first emergency call in 1876 •	• **Great Britain**
Person who connected two phones using a switchboard •	• **Utah**
Country that first used a standard emergency phone number •	• **Alexander Graham Bell**
State that had the first 9-1-1 call in the U.S. •	• **dispatcher**
State that has the Valley Emergency Communications Center •	• **Alabama**
Person who answers 9-1-1 calls and decides how to help •	• **telephone operator**

Lesson 102

Fighting Fires, Saving Lives

These words are all related to the work that EMTs, paramedics, and firefighters do. Some of the words are scrambled below. Unscramble them to complete the sentences. You will not use all of the words

Firefighters in Colorado Practice Putting Out a Car Fire

ambulance
bandage
communication
department
ladder
training
trucks
uniform

1. An EMT receives about 150 hours of ________________.
   NARNITIG

2. An __________________ is like a mini-hospital.
   EANMLBUAC

3. Emergency workers use ___________________________ equipment.
   OTNMUCAMICINO

4. Pierce Manufacturing is a company that makes fire ___________.
   SRTKCU

5. Turnout pants are part of a firefighter's ________________.
   NFMUROI

Lesson 103

Friends and Protectors

Look at the law enforcement patches on pages 663 and 664. Find the patch that matches each of the patch shapes below. In each patch outline, write the name of the state from which the matching patch comes.

Ready for the Weather

Using the following list of states and the symbols on the map, write the name of the state that matches each statement below. You may need an atlas or U.S. map for help in identifying states.

Arizona Florida Hawaii New York Oklahoma

1. This state has frequent serious tornadoes. ____________________
2. This state has frequent hurricanes. ____________________
3. This state has a high average annual rainfall. ____________________
4. This state has a high average of sunny days. ____________________
5. This state has several cities that rank near the top for average snowfall per year. ____________________

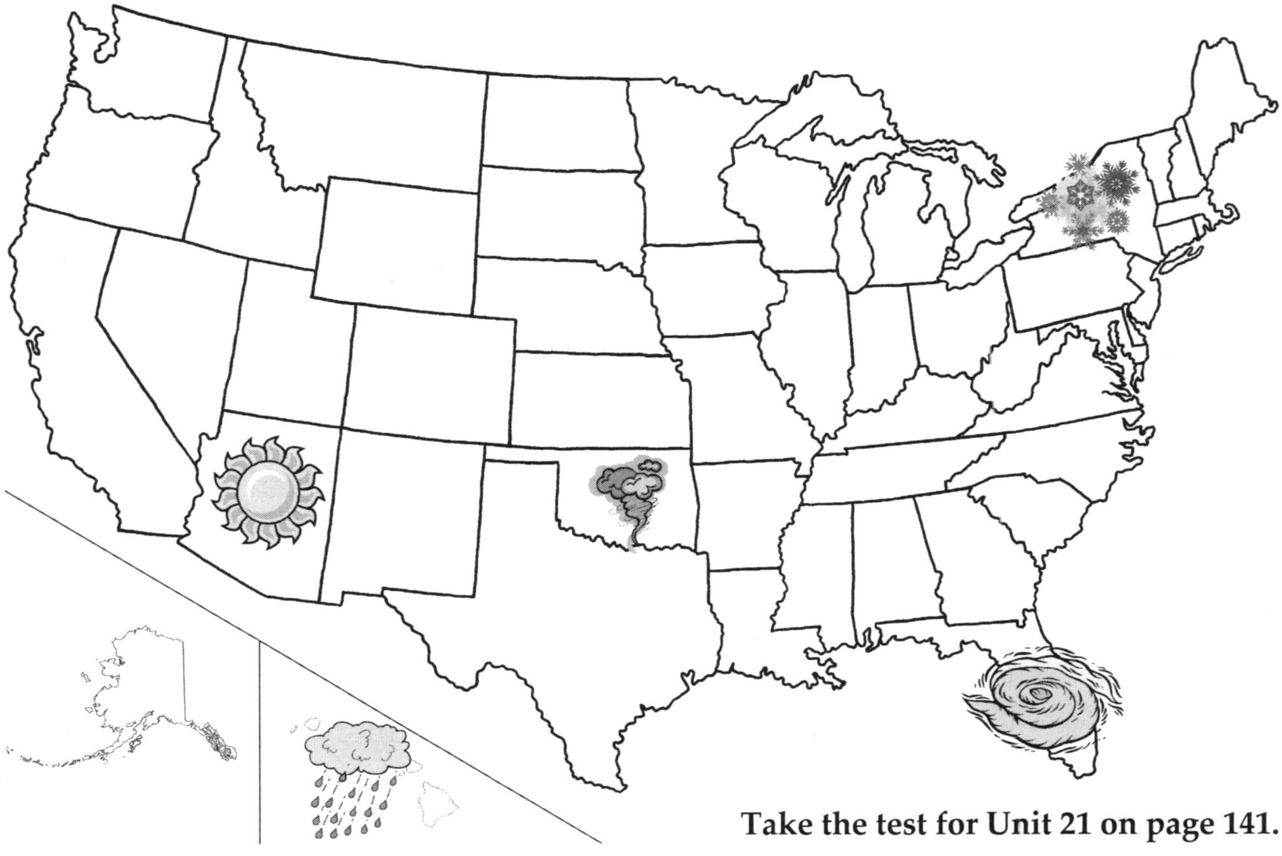

Take the test for Unit 21 on page 141.

Justice for All

Complete this crossword puzzle.

Across

1. The group of citizens who listen to the evidence in a court case and decide on the outcome
3. A person who is accused of a crime
5. A spoken promise
7. A person who has personal knowledge of the evidence in a court case

Down

2. The person who is in charge of what happens in a courtroom
4. If a court decides that someone has done something wrong and should be punished, that person is said to be _____.
6. An assistant to the judge in the courtroom
8. Another name for a lawyer who represents a defendant or a plaintiff

A gavel is a symbol of the judge's authority in the courtroom. The judge uses it to get the attention of people in the courtroom and to emphasize important announcements.

Lesson 107

Crime and Punishment

Find these terms from the lesson in the puzzle below.

accused
attorney
bail
civil
criminal
due process
fine
incarceration
judge
jury
justice
magistrate
parole
plea bargain
probation
prosecutor
protection
public defender
restitution
rights
sentence
settlement
trial
witness

Some convicted criminals are sent to prison.

Q	L	D	K	J	H	G	M	E	A	T	T	O	R	N	E	Y	T	Y	U	I	I	U	P
W	[	U	D	E	W	F	A	R	F	W	S	E	T	T	L	E	M	E	N	T	N	Y	L
R	P	E	E	C	A	F	G	T	G	I	Z	X	S	X	Z	P	R	R	T	E	C	T	E
E	O	P	R	F	C	R	I	G	H	T	S	C	D	S	C	R	I	M	I	N	A	L	A
S	I	R	T	D	C	V	S	F	H	N	U	V	F	E	A	O	E	B	V	B	R	A	B
T	U	O	Y	J	U	S	T	I	C	E	Y	B	G	T	S	B	W	S	S	X	C	Z	A
I	Y	C	E	F	S	T	R	W	J	S	T	F	H	Y	D	A	A	E	W	C	E	F	R
T	T	E	D	D	E	R	A	E	K	S	R	B	J	U	F	T	F	N	J	U	R	Y	G
U	R	S	C	S	D	W	T	R	L	F	E	A	K	I	G	I	D	T	R	I	A	L	A
T	C	S	S	Z	T	E	E	T	P	D	F	I	N	E	H	O	Y	E	R	S	T	H	I
I	I	E	J	U	D	G	E	Y	O	S	W	L	L	O	J	N	T	N	T	V	I	J	N
O	V	W	R	W	P	R	O	S	E	C	U	T	O	R	K	C	R	C	Y	F	O	T	V
N	I	P	A	R	O	L	E	U	I	A	Q	N	M	P	L	D	E	E	U	G	N	R	R
E	L	T	T	E	Y	R	P	U	B	L	I	C	D	E	F	E	N	D	E	R	W	E	Y
A	B	C	D	P	R	O	T	E	C	T	I	O	N	E	F	G	H	I	J	K	L	M	N

Chuck Colson and Prison Fellowship

Follow the directions below to identify the correct match for each statement. Not all of the answers at the bottom of the page will be used.

1. Draw a circle around the name of the President for whom Chuck Colson worked.
2. Draw a diamond around the name of the office and hotel complex that was the site of a burglary.
3. Draw a rectangle around the name of the Prison Fellowship program that helps churches, community groups, and individuals reach out to former inmates.
4. Draw a star above the name of the Prison Fellowship program that provides gifts for the children of people in prison.
5. Draw a line under the organization that works to promote Biblical standards of justice.

Mariott

2,000

Ronald Reagan

Gerald Ford

Hilton

Justice Fellowship

Angel Tree

Richard Nixon

Out4Life

Watergate

200

Lesson 109

The Supreme Court

Answer these math problems based on information from the lesson.

1. The British burned the U.S. Capitol in 1814, forcing the Supreme Court to meet in another location. The Supreme Court returned to the capitol in 1819. How many years did it meet in another location?

2. Each frieze in the Supreme Court Chamber is forty feet long. There are four friezes. What is the total length of all four?

3. If all nine Supreme Court justices played basketball together and each person scored 12 points, what would be the total number of points scored?

4. If the Supreme Court agreed to hear 80 cases in one year, and the justices heard two cases per day, how many days would they need to hear all 80 cases?

5. If six out of nine Supreme Court justices agree on the decision in a particular case, what would that fraction be reduced to the lowest terms?

Take the test for Unit 22 on page 142.

America's Free Economy

Circle the correct answer beneath each question.

1. What is the name of the tax that is added to the purchase price of a product in most states?

   a. sales tax   b. income tax   c. Medicare tax

2. What is the term for moving products from one location to another?

   a. retribution   b. dissolution   c. distribution

3. What is the name for the money that a bank pays to its customers when they put money in the bank?

   a. penalty   b. interest   c. deposit

4. What is the name for the type of economy in which the government tells everyone what to do?

   a. free market   b. planned   c. super

5. Which Federal executive department oversees the money that the government collects and spends?

   a. Treasury   b. State   c. Homeland Security

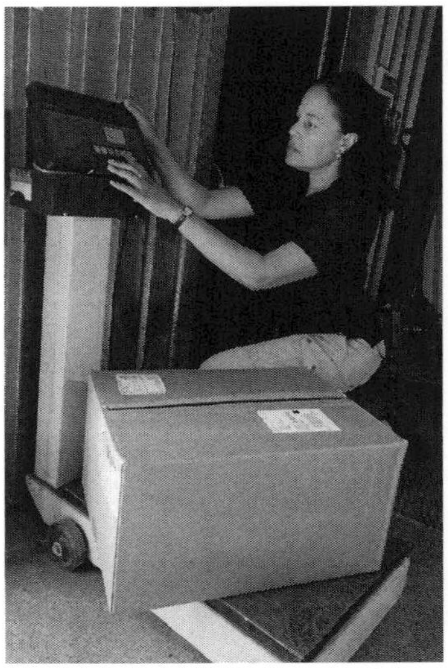

Lesson 112

The Life of Dollar Bill

Listed below are twelve things related to money along with the twelve Federal Reserve Banks. The locations of these banks are on the map. Draw a line from each money drawing to the location of the bank listed with that drawing. The first one is completed for you.

1. Five Dollar Bill — St. Louis Federal Reserve Bank — H 8
2. Dollar Sign — San Francisco Federal Reserve Bank — L 12
3. Wallet — Dallas Federal Reserve Bank — K 11
4. Cents Sign — Richmond Federal Reserve Bank — E 5
5. Antique Cash register — New York City Federal Reserve Bank — B 2
6. Bank building — Cleveland Federal Reserve Bank — D 4
7. The Motto of the U.S.A., "In God We Trust" — Minneapolis Federal Reserve Bank —I 9
8. Piggy bank —Atlanta Federal Reserve Bank — F 6
9. Purse — Kansas City, MO Federal Reserve Bank — J 10
10. ATM — Philadelphia Federal Reserve Bank — C 3
11. Coin Purse — Boston Federal Reserve Bank — A 1
12. Safe — Chicago Federal Reserve Bank — G 7

In God We Trust

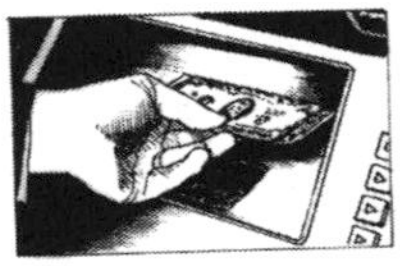

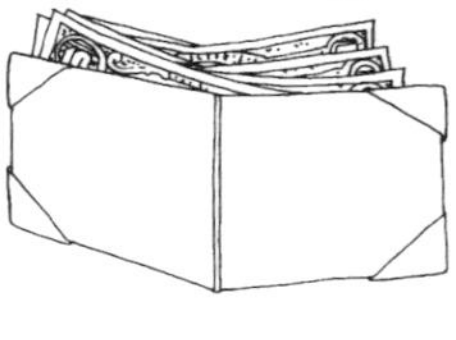

From Kernel to Cookie

Listed below are twelve of the steps needed for a kernel of wheat to become part of a cookie. Put them in order by writing the numbers 1-12 in the ovals. The first one has been completed for you.

- ( ) Scientists check and grade stored wheat kernels.
- ( ) Flour is sealed in paper bags.
- ( ) Wheat sprouts after it is planted and then lies dormant through the winter.
- ( ) Flour is stocked on grocery store shelves.
- (1) A farmer plants his wheat field.
- ( ) Wheat is placed in a holding area of a grain elevator.
- ( ) Flour is made into cookies.
- ( ) The farmer harvests his field with a combine.
- ( ) Wheat is cleaned for milling.
- ( ) Wheat grows two to four feet tall during the spring.
- ( ) Nutrients are added to white flour.
- ( ) Wheat heads bend over or "nod."

Lesson 114

How We Pay for Government

On the pie chart below:

1. Color the amount that the Federal government makes from customs GREEN.
2. Color the amount that the Federal government makes from tax on profit of corporations YELLOW.
3. Color the amount that the Federal government makes from personal income tax PURPLE.
4. Color the amount that the Federal government makes from excise taxes BLACK.
5. Color the amount that the Federal government makes from taxes on gifts and inheritances ORANGE.
6. Color the amount that the Federal government makes from taxes for Social Security and Medicare GRAY.

On the graph at right:

7. Color the total revenue of the Federal government BLUE.
8. Color the total spending of the Federal government RED.

U.S. Revenue and Spending in 2011

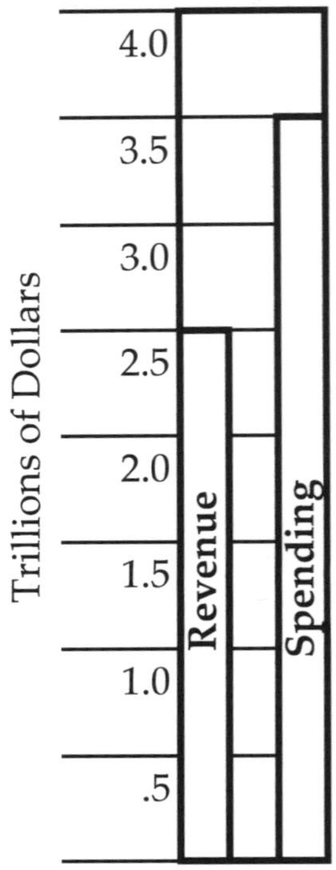

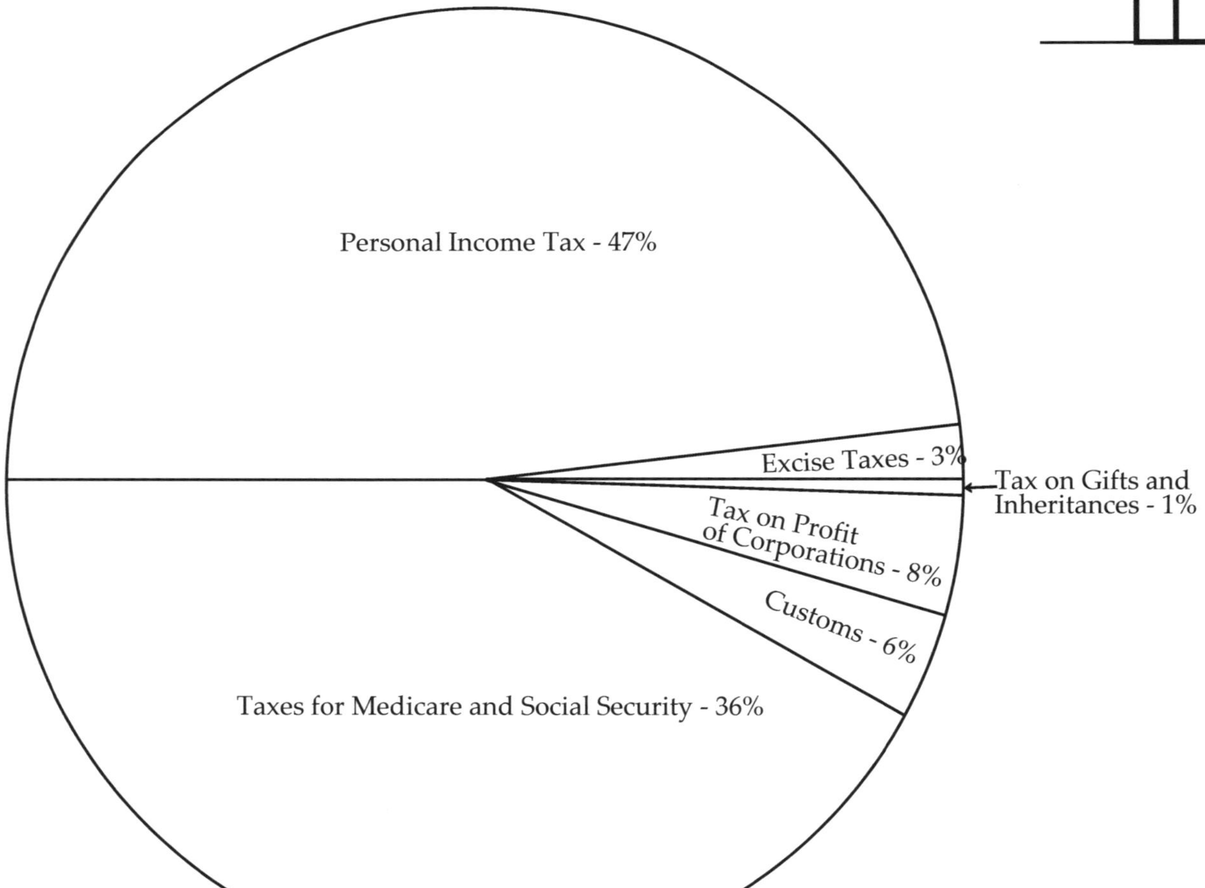

Take the test for Unit 23 on page 143.

America's God-Given Resources

Using the following list of states and the symbols on the map, write the name of the state that matches each statement below. You may need an atlas or U.S. map for help in identifying states.

Arizona Arkansas Maine Nevada
North Dakota New Mexico Wyoming

1. Hunting provides food. It is popular in ______________.
2. Hoover Dam, on the border between ________________ and ________________, uses the Colorado River to produce energy.
3. Coal mining in ________________ supplies power plants.
4. ______________________________ has become the second-largest oil-producing state.
5. __________________________ is a good place to collect solar power.
6. Over half of ____________________ is covered with timber.

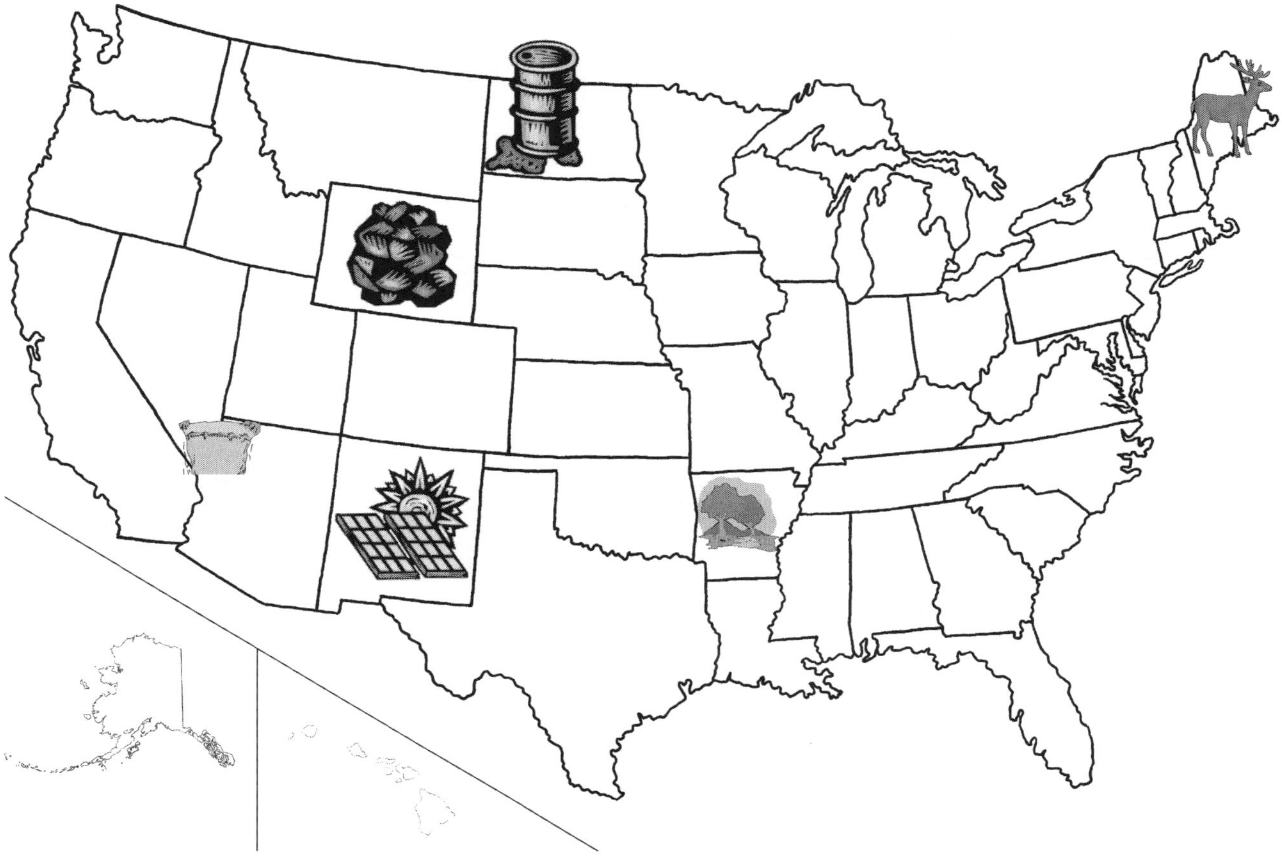

Power to Run America

Unscramble these sources of electricity that people in the United States use.

____

TREOCDERHLYIC

____

LROAS

____

NDWI

____

LOCA

____

LNERUAC

____

UNTRALA SGA

____

OTRHEGALME

Roscoe Wind Farm

Draw a picture of a modern wind farm. Fill the horizon with one large windmill or several smaller windmills.

Lesson 119

Government and Agriculture

Draw a line from each word on the left to the matching description on the right.

parity •	• **a fuel that is often made from corn in the United States**
surplus •	• **weed killer**
ethanol •	• **a price for farm products set by the government**
SNAP •	• **Supplemental Nutrition Assistance Program**
herbicide •	• **a government program that encouraged Americans to live and work on farmland**
pesticide •	• **food purchased by the government to keep prices higher**
Homestead Act •	• **bug killer**

Take the test for Unit 24 on page 144.

American Technology

Fill in the blank in each sentence, using the words below. To find out one of the blessings that promotes American technology, write the underlined letters in order in the blanks at lower right.

INVENTED COMPUTER SPACE LIGHTNING
BELL EDISON WAR IMAGE WRIGHT AUTHOR

 1. Benjamin Franklin invented the __________ rod.	 2. Alexander Graham __________ invented the telephone.	 3. Thomas __________ invented the phonograph.
 4. Mark Twain was the first __________ to have his manuscript typed.	 5. Cyrus McCormick __________ the McCormick reaper in 1831.	 6. Wilbur and Orville __________ first flew their Flyer at Kitty Hawk, North Carolina.
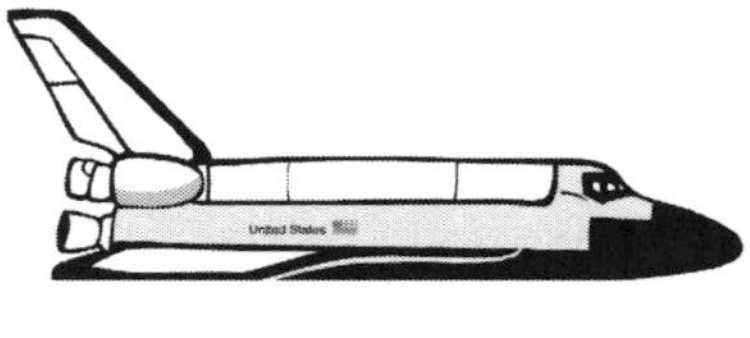 7. NASA launched and landed the first __________ Shuttle in 1981.	 8. God created human beings in His __________.	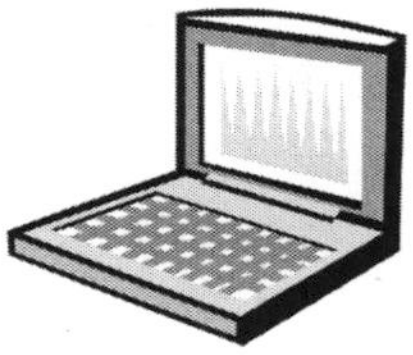 9. Bill Gates is a ______________ software pioneer.
 10. Lincoln used Morse's telegraph to transmit messages during the Civil __________.	___ ___ ___ ___ ___ ___ ___ ___ ___ ___ ___ ___ ___ ___ ___ ___ ___ ___ ___	

Lesson 122

From Tin Cans to Smart Phones

Complete this crossword puzzle.

Across

1. God created sound __________.
3. Almon Strowger and his associates developed the automatic switchboard and the rotary __________.
5. The first person-to-person __________ message was sent in 1993.
7. Bell received a U.S. __________ for his telephone.
9. In the past, telephone calls had to be manually connected by an __________.
11. The __________ is a network of computer networks.
13. The telephone was born when Alexander Graham Bell spoke through a device to his assistant Thomas A. __________.

Down

2. God created people with the __________ to communicate.
4. The iPhone produced by Apple is an example of a __________.
6. With every new stage in the history of the __________, people have to make decisions about how they will use them.
8. Telephones are important because of the need for __________ to communicate with each other.
10. Bell's original company eventually became the __________ Telephone & Telegraph Company (AT&T).
12. The first handheld __________ phone, developed by Motorola, weighed 2 1/2 pounds.

The Travels of a Piece of Mail

To find out the years of significant events in postal history, do these subtraction problems which use actual ZIP codes of American towns.

1. Little Ferry, New Jersey 07643
   Troy, Vermont - 05868
   U.S. Post office began: ______

2. Rock Hill, New York 12775
   Tappan, New York - 10983
   Post Office Department created: ______

3) Vandalia, Ohio 45377
   Blakeslee, Ohio - 43505
   Postmaster General joined President's Cabinet in: ______

4) Morven, North Carolina 28119
   Macfarlen, West Virginia - 26148
   Post Office Department became independent agency: ______

5. Alamo, Nevada 89001
   Cochiti Lake, New Mexico - 87083
   The first mail was delivered by airplane in: ______

6. Parrott, Georgia 39877
   Knoxville, Tennessee - 37914
   The ZIP code system was introduced in: ______

7. Fort Totten, North Dakota 58335
   Laporte, Minnesota - 56461
   The Universal Postal Union was established in: ______

8) University Place, Washington 98467
   FPO, AP (Armed Forces Pacific) - 96620
   First Federal postage stamp issued: ______

Put the letters in the correct bags. Draw a line from each word to the bag that is missing that word. Also draw a line from the three or four letter-acronym that represents the words on the bag.

Voice of America

Some of the words of the Voice of America charter are underlined below. Find those words in the word search.

The Voice of America will serve as a consistently **reliable** and **authoritative** source of **news**. VOA news will be **accurate**, **objective**, and **comprehensive**.

The VOA will represent **America**, not any single segment of American **society**, and will therefore present a **balanced** and comprehensive projection of **significant** American **thought** and institutions.

VOA will present the **policies** of the United States **clearly** and **effectively**, and will also present **responsible** **discussions** and **opinion** on these policies.

U	N	C	L	E	S	A	M	C	O	M	P	R	E	H	E	N	S	I	V	E	A	B	R
A	B	C	D	E	F	G	H	I	J	K	L	M	N	O	P	B	Q	R	S	T	U	V	E
E	F	F	E	C	T	I	V	E	L	Y	A	L	L	C	D	A	W	X	Y	Z	E	J	S
W	A	S	H	I	N	G	T	O	N	F	G	H	I	J	C	L	E	A	R	L	Y	E	P
A	D	A	M	S	N	A	T	I	O	N	K	N	L	M	N	A	O	P	Q	R	S	F	O
A	U	T	H	O	R	I	T	A	T	I	V	E	T	U	V	N	W	X	Y	Z	A	F	N
C	B	H	L	S	E	Y	E	K	Q	A	W	W	B	D	F	C	J	M	R	Y	Z	E	S
C	C	O	M	T	L	Z	F	L	R	M	X	S	O	C	I	E	T	Y	S	O	A	R	I
U	D	U	N	U	I	A	G	M	S	E	Y	A	C	E	G	D	K	N	T	P	B	S	B
R	E	G	O	V	A	B	H	N	T	R	F	O	R	D	H	I	L	O	U	I	C	O	L
A	F	H	P	O	B	J	E	C	T	I	V	E	J	U	S	T	I	C	E	N	D	N	E
T	G	T	Q	W	L	C	I	O	U	C	L	I	B	E	R	T	Y	P	V	I	E	I	M
E	H	K	R	X	E	D	J	P	V	A	Z	D	I	S	C	U	S	S	I	O	N	S	N
L	I	P	O	L	I	C	I	E	S	H	C	L	I	N	T	O	N	Q	W	N	F	J	O
K	E	N	N	E	D	Y	N	I	X	O	N	J	A	C	K	S	O	N	X	H	G	K	P
J	I	S	I	G	N	I	F	I	C	A	N	T	R	O	O	S	E	V	E	L	T	L	Q

Take the test for Unit 25 on page 145.

Americans on the Move

Circle the correct answer beneath each question. Look at the photos in Lesson 126 for help.

1) Which state welcome sign has words in English and French?

a. Rhode Island b. Louisiana c. Wyoming

2) In which state is the New River Gorge Bridge?

a. West Virginia b. Oregon c. Texas

3) Where is the southernmost point in the continental United States?

a. Georgia b. California c. Florida

4) Which state has a village called Port of Galilee?

a. Rhode Island b. Montana c. Virginia

5) Where can you see a mile marker from the Cumberland Road?

a. Oregon b. Georgia c. Ohio

6) Through which state does Interstate 5 pass?

a. New York b. Oregon c. Kentucky

7) Where was the world's first major offshore runway built?

a. Hawaii b. California c. Washington, D.C.

Lesson 127

How to Build a Road

Read these statements and put each word in ALL CAPS in its correct location in the puzzle below.

City and county OFFICIALS work with the Department of TRANSPORTATION to plan new roads. Civil ENGINEERS DESIGN the road, taking into consideration SAFETY for drivers and the environment. A private company builds the road.

The ROADBED is prepared with SAND, ROCK, and gravel. ASPHALT paving material is used to create the top layer of the road. Painted lines, GUARDRAILS, and signs help keep people safe while driving.

Traveling Together on Mass Transit

Answer these math problems related to mass transit.

1. Yosef rides the bus ten times and pays 50 cents for each ride. How much money has he spent?

2. Kiran is a bus driver. He makes twelve round trips of his route per day. His bus carries a total of 1200 passengers during one day. What is the average number of passengers per trip?

3. Erika gets on the subway at 7:45 a.m. and gets off at 9:15 a.m., how long has she been riding?

4. Taylor started her journey on the first trolley. She ended her journey on her fourth trolley. How many times did she change trolleys?

5. Miguel rides on a light rail line twice a day, five days per week. He does this for 50 weeks per year. How many total trips in a year has he taken?

Lesson 129

Working in Transportation

Find these occupations in the puzzle below. If a word is listed more than once, it is in the puzzle more than once. Hyphens are omitted in the puzzle.

Secretary of Transportation

School Crossing Guard

Heavy Equipment Operator

Air Traffic Controller

Tractor-Trailer Driver

Adopt-a-Highway Program Coordinator

Locomotive Engineer

City Traffic Engineer

Cargo Handler

P	G	M	O	D	E	Q	R	A	C	T	R	A	C	T	O	R	T	R	A	I	L	E	R
E	U	R	W	V	B	T	Y	U	H	G	O	F	R	E	W	D	A	S	C	Z	D	F	C
T	A	C	X	V	A	D	O	P	T	A	H	I	G	H	W	A	Y	F	S	E	E	D	I
R	R	C	X	S	I	W	E	E	N	G	I	N	E	E	R	N	B	E	C	W	R	W	T
L	D	Q	E	E	R	H	D	V	M	B	V	C	X	S	W	C	V	D	H	E	A	V	Y
O	R	T	S	C	D	A	S	F	N	C	A	R	G	O	E	O	C	O	O	W	P	E	L
C	C	R	T	R	A	N	S	P	O	R	T	A	T	I	O	N	F	P	O	D	O	N	K
O	S	A	C	E	V	D	C	H	K	O	R	W	C	Q	R	T	E	E	L	C	L	G	J
M	D	F	F	T	C	L	V	T	I	S	T	E	F	W	F	R	T	R	A	F	F	I	C
O	T	F	D	A	X	E	F	Y	U	S	F	R	V	D	V	O	E	A	R	W	K	N	H
T	F	I	A	R	S	R	E	Q	U	I	P	M	E	N	T	L	C	T	C	R	K	E	G
I	V	C	C	Y	W	T	R	B	F	N	N	B	V	C	Y	L	S	O	D	E	J	E	F
V	C	Q	E	U	T	Y	P	R	O	G	R	A	M	D	T	E	D	R	I	V	E	R	D
E	A	W	C	O	O	R	D	I	N	A	T	O	R	E	R	R	Q	R	D	C	Z	X	V

Take the test for Unit 26 on page 146.

People Helping People

Fit these words into the statements below. You will write some letters in boxes and others on lines. The first one has been completed for you. When you are finished filling in the blanks with letters, write each boxed letter in order in the blanks in the statement in the oval at the bottom of the page.

GOD SUNDAY BRADY HEART NEED GOOD
ROOSEVELT TRUTH OTHERS HELP ALASKA

Jesus had a [H] [E] A R T of compassion for each person.

Let us do [ ] __ [ ] __ to all people.

Let us love in deed and [ ] __ __ __ [ ].

Christians in Britain began [ ] __ __ __ __ __ schools in the 1780s.

Helping __ __ __ __ [ ] [ ] is a satisfying thing to do.

The Good Samaritan responded to the __ [ ] __ __ he saw.

Volunteers __ __ __ __ communities in practical ways.

Theodore __ __ __ __ __ __ __ [ ] __ Sr. cared about the poor.

Roosevelt helped a boy named John __ __ __ __ __.

Brady served as Governor of the __ __ __ __ __ __ Territory.

When we do things for the poor, we honor [ ] [ ] [ ].

__ __ L P I N __ __ __ __ __ E R __
__ E F L E C T __ T H __
__ O V E O F __ __ __.

Lesson 132

Federal Helping Programs

Use colored pencils to follow the instructions below.

1. Draw a line of green arrows to the Federal program that began in 1912.	Medicare
2. Draw a blue dotted line to the department of the Federal government that oversees about 300 programs.	Department of Health and Human Services
3. Draw a pink wavy line to the program that funds food and nutritional education to expectant and new mothers and to children to age five.	Department of Housing and Urban Development
4. Draw a line of yellow bananas to the program that helps low-income families purchase food.	National Institutes of Health
5. Draw a line of stair steps to the government program that provides assistance to low-income families in renting an apartment.	Centers for Disease Control and Prevention
6. Draw a line of green dollar signs to the program that helps families acquire a loan for a home with a low down payment.	Social Security
7. Draw a line of golf clubs to the program that provides a minimum level of income for retired persons.	Children's Bureau
8. Draw a line of adhesive bandages to the program that provides health care to elderly Americans.	Women, Infants, and Children
9. Draw a line of check marks to the program that collects and publishes information about health.	Federal Housing Administration
10. Draw a line of question marks to the program that provides money for medical research.	Supplemental Nutrition Assistance Program

State and Local Helping Agencies

Use the secret code to fill in the blanks of Isaiah 58:6-7. Remember that these words express the desire of our Father in heaven in His own words.

✎=A ❄=B 💧=C ④=D ❀=E ⌘=F ↑=G 🕐=H
★=I ⦿=J ⮝=K ☼=L ☺=M 🔔=N 📖=O 🕯=P ☎=Q
✂=R ⁂=S ◈=T ❿=U △=V ◆=W ✖=X ⬣=Y ✋=Z

"Is this not the fast which ___ choose,
★

To loosen the bonds of ______________________________,
◆ ★ 💧 ⮝ ❀ ④ 🔔 ❀ ⁂ ⁂

To undo the bands of the ____________,
⬣ 📖 ⮝ ❀

And to let the ___________________________ go free
📖 🕯 🕯 ✂ ❀ ⁂ ⁂ ❀ ④

And _________________ every yoke?
❄ ✂ ❀ ✎ ⮝

Is it not to _____________ your bread with the ______________
④ ★ △ ★ ④ ❀ 🕐 ❿ 🔔 ↑ ✂ ⬣

And bring the ___________________________ poor into the house;
🕐 📖 ☺ ❀ ☼ ❀ ⁂ ⁂

When you see the naked, to ______________ him;
💧 📖 △ ❀ ✂

And not to ___________ yourself from your own ___________?"
🕐 ★ ④ ❀ ⌘ ☼ ❀ ⁂ 🕐

Lesson 134

Private Groups That Help Others

Each statement below is missing one word. Draw a line from the statement to the light bulb that has the correct missing word(s).

1. The people of the _______ give the most money in charitable donations.	2. Americans give the most to __________ organizations.	3. William Booth started preaching in ____________ in 1852.	4. William Booth began ______________.	5. The first Salvation Army meeting in America was held in ____________.	6. Volunteer bell ringers collect money for The Salvation Army at ____________.
7. The name of the Civitan Club is based on the Latin word *civatas* which means ____________.	8. In its early years, Civitan International provided _________ for children with disabilities.	9. ___________ helps low- to moderate-income families own their own home.	10. ___________ founded the world's first food bank in 1967.	11. American President _____________ made a tremendous impact by feeding the hungry.	12. __________ provides daily meals for over one million older Americans.

Take the test for Unit 27 on page 147.

The Education of a President

Complete this crossword puzzle about President Theodore Roosevelt.

Across

1. Where did he go to college?
3. In what Territory did he own a ranch?
5. What was his father's nickname?
7. To what museum did he donate 250 of his animal specimens?
9. What was his mother's nickname?

Down

2. What sickness did he have as a child?
4. He liked poetry from what country?
6. From what country did his ancestors immigrate to America?
8. What sport did he pursue even as Governor of New York?
10. When he was ten and fourteen, his family went where?

The 1902 cartoon by Clifford Berryman below depicts Theodore Roosevelt refusing to shoot a captured bear during a hunting trip. The cartoon inspired New York entrepreneur Morris Michtom to create a stuffed animal. Michtom called it a Teddy Bear with President Roosevelt's permission.

Lesson 137

The Education of a Nation

Draw a line from each word or phrase on the left to the matching description on the right.

Oxford	**the first state to require school attendance**
Massachusetts	**public schools that do not have to follow typical rules and regulations**
G. I. Bill	**the approximate number of children who are homeschooled in the U.S.**
charter schools	**one of the first universities in England**
two million	**U.S. President who was an assistant teacher at a school for the blind**
Blue Bird	**a program designed to help World War II veterans attend college**
Cleveland	**a Georgia company that manufactures school buses**

A Home for American Art

Circle the correct answer beneath each question.

1. Where is the Tin Man statue located that is pictured in the lesson?

   a. Alaska b. Arkansas c. Alabama

2. What is the modern name for the country where John James Audubon was born?

   a. France b. Costa Rica c. Haiti

3. What did Audubon's book *Viviparous Quadrupeds of North America* illustrate?

   a. birds b. animals c. fish

4. Who created the World War I poster illustrated in the lesson?

   a. Howard Pyle b. Emile Marghab c. Harvey Dunn

5. Oscar Howe designed art for what building in Mitchell, South Dakota?

   a. Corn Palace b. Chocolate Hut c. Gingerbread House

6. Where is the Georgia O'Keeffe Museum located?

   a. Wisconsin b. New York c. New Mexico

7. Who inspired Anne Windfohr Marion to donate money to start a museum in honor of Georgia O'Keefe?

   a. Her mother b. Her sister c. Her father

Lesson 139

A Year of Performing Arts

These words are all related to the performing arts mentioned in the story in this lesson. Write each word in its correct location in the puzzle below.

Ballet
Band
Choir
Comedian
Concert
Folk
Oratorio
Orchestra
Play
Recital
Rehearsal

Take the test for Unit 28 on page 148.

How Americans Preserve History

In each of the following sentences, one word is scrambled. Unscramble the words.

1. The IDLRWAL ____________ Hotel was called "The Hotel of Presidents."

2. The Washington TMENNMUO ______________ was opened to the public in 1888.

3. At Hasbrouck House, George Washington created the Badge of TLYIAIRM __________________ Merit.

4. The American Association for ATTES _______ and Local History began in 1940.

5. Plimoth LNNOPITTTAA __________________ is a living history museum.

6. The ADEELFR __________________ Writers' Project preserved the personal stories of those who had been born into slavery.

7. The United States OLTPAS _____________ Service issues commemorative stamps.

8. The National IGSEERRT __________________ of Historic Places is a list of places recognized as worthy of preservation.

9. One-fourth of the places named National Historic Landmarks are in Pennsylvania, TTSSSUAAHCESM ___________________ and New York.

10. Many people study ANEELYGGO _______________ to learn their own history.

Preservation work at the Willard Hotel

Lesson 142

Saving George Washington's Home

Use a calculator to fill in the dates of this Timeline of Mount Vernon. Write the answers to the math questions in the blanks to the right of the problems.

Timeline of Mount Vernon

78 x 30 - 597 =	________ ←	After their father's death, George Washington's brother Lawrence inherited the Mount Vernon estate.
3000 – 2566 + 1327 =	________ ←	George Washington became the owner of Mount Vernon.
4974 ÷ 6 + 968 =	________ ←	George Washington retired to Mount Vernon after his second term as President.
8966 + 3219 – 10386 =	________ ←	George Washington died at Mount Vernon and was buried on the estate.
5780 ÷ 20 + 1564 =	________ ←	Louisa Bird Cunningham wrote a letter to her daughter suggesting that the women of his country should preserve the home of George Washington.
9366 ÷ 2 – 2830 =	________ ←	Ann Pamela Cunningham founded the Mount Vernon Ladies' Association.
90 x 22 – 120 =	________ ←	The Mount Vernon Ladies' Association took over operations at Mount Vernon.
8901 + 1006 – 8033 =	________ ←	Ann Pamela Cunningham resigned from leading the Mount Vernon Ladies' Association.

America's State Parks

Complete the crossword puzzle.

Across

1. The fifty __________ have about 6,600 state parks.
3. The Civilian Conservation __________ constructed many state parks in the 1930s.
5. Niagara __________ State Park is the oldest park in the country.
7. State parks need ______________ to clear trails, repair buildings, and pick up litter.
9. Seventeen states offer yurts as an alternative to tents for __________.
11. State parks preserve many important historic __________ from state and national history.

Down

2. State parks welcome over 700 million ________ each year.
4. Adirondack Park covers over six million __________ in New York.
6. Water activities such as fishing, swimming, and ______________ are popular at state parks.
8. Hikers can enjoy over 41,000 miles of ____________ in America's state parks.
10. State parks are great locations for special __________, such as parties, family reunions, and weddings.

Lesson 144

Working in Tourism

Draw a poster which is designed to tell international tourists that the USA is a great vacation destination.

Take the test for Unit 29 on page 149.

Serving in Three Branches of the Federal Government

In the left column are positions held by the people in the right column. Draw a line from each list of positions to the person who held them.

Senator Secretary of the Treasury Chief Justice •	• **Lucius Quintus Cincinnatus Lamar II**
Representative Secretary of the Treasury Chief Justice •	• **Salmon P. Chase**
District Court Judge Senator Ambassador to the UN •	• **James F. Byrnes**
Representative Secretary of State Chief Justice •	• **John Marshall**
Representative Secretary of the Interior Associate Justice •	• **James L. Buckley**
Representative & Senator Associate Justice Secretary of State •	• **Fred Vinson**
Senator Head of Radio Free Europe Court of Appeals Judge •	• **Warren Austin**

A Civics Day In the USA

Find these Federal government occupations in the puzzle below.

Agent
Ambassador
Curator
Governor
Intern
Justice
Legislator
Nurse
Officer
Operator
Ranger
Soldier

A	S	X	Z	C	D	E	R	F	G	T	G	Y	U	I	P	L	J	N	G
R	V	B	A	M	B	A	S	S	A	D	O	R	C	S	W	R	Y	Z	A
A	C	N	G	Y	Y	T	B	W	E	D	V	S	W	A	N	E	B	J	S
N	X	M	E	U	S	R	V	X	R	F	E	A	Q	Z	U	F	G	U	D
G	Z	K	N	I	O	E	C	D	C	U	R	A	T	O	R	D	Y	S	F
E	A	J	T	O	L	W	X	C	T	G	N	C	X	W	S	X	F	T	G
R	I	H	T	P	D	S	D	W	Y	H	O	X	A	E	E	C	H	I	R
D	N	L	E	G	I	S	L	A	T	O	R	S	R	F	V	V	B	C	Y
V	T	G	R	L	E	D	E	D	U	J	E	E	O	F	F	I	C	E	R
E	E	F	E	K	R	F	T	B	I	K	R	W	N	S	C	G	V	A	B
X	R	D	W	O	P	E	R	A	T	O	R	D	B	X	S	F	C	S	F
Q	N	S	A	J	H	G	Y	U	O	L	G	B	V	C	V	B	E	W	E

A Civics Day In Your Town

Read this list of words. Some of them are scrambled in the five sentences. Unscramble them to complete the sentences. You will not use all of the words.

clerk
councilman
director
doctor
firefighter
interpreter
judge
mayor
nurse
teacher

1. A ________________ explains things to the jury during a trial.
DUJEG

2. The city ________________ often speaks at local ceremonies.
ORAMY

3. Someone who helps people talk to each other when they don't speak the same language is an ________________________________.
RPTITREENRE

4. A ______________________ decorates her classroom.
HRTEAEC

5. Sick people can see a ___________________ at a clinic.
TRODCO

Lesson 149

Uncle Sam and You

Color these words and draw illustrations of people doing what it says.

Love Your

Neighbor

As Yourself

Take the test for Unit 30 on page 150.

Unit 1 Test

Indicate whether each statement is true or false.

________ 1. Auburn University Chapel was built with bricks made by Native Americans.

________ 2. Maranatha Baptist Church in Plains, Georgia, is the home church of Jimmy and Rosalynn Carter.

________ 3. Florida was the first state to ratify the Constitution.

________ 4. Ohio was the first state admitted in the nineteenth century.

________ 5. Texas was the first state west of the Mississippi River.

________ 6. California became a state in 1850 after a gold rush the previous year.

________ 7. Alaska and Hawaii became states in 1959.

________ 8. Bagel is a word we get from Yiddish.

________ 9. We got the word hamburger from French.

________ 10. Squash is a word that came to us from the Swedish language.

Unit 2 Test

Put the letter of the correct answer in the blank beside the number.

_____ 1. He spoke at the opening of the Emancipation Proclamation Exhibit at the National Archives in 1963.
a. Abraham Lincoln b. Herbert Hoover c. Robert Kennedy

_____ 2. He laid the cornerstone for the National Archives in 1933.
a. Herbert Hoover b. Franklin Roosevelt c. Barry Faulkner

_____ 3. In its display at the National Archives, the Constitution covers this many sheets of parchment.
a. One b. Two c. Four

_____ 4. In 1774 the Continental Congress met in:
a. Boston b. Philadelphia c. New York

_____ 5. On July 4, 1776, the Continental Congress:
a. approved the final version of the Declaration of Independence
b. declared war on Great Britain
c. finished the Constitution

_____ 6. On August 2, 1776, most members of the Continental Congress:
a. resigned from the Congress and joined the Continental Army
b. signed the parchment copy of the Declaration of Independence
c. arrived in Boston to begin Congress' work

_____ 7. The Preamble to the U.S. Constitution says that the Constitution was ordained and established by:
a. We, the people of the United States
b. Congress
c. a majority of states

_____ 8. The Preamble says that the Constitution was established to secure the blessings of liberty:
a. to all people around the world
b. to that generation
c. to ourselves and our posterity

_____ 9. The First Amendment to the U.S. Constitution says that Congress cannot prohibit the free exercise of:
a. Christianity b. religion c. self-defense

_____ 10. According to the Fifth Amendment, without due process of law no one can be deprived of life, liberty, or:
a. property b. happiness c. newspapers

Unit 3 Test

Answer the following questions.

What are the three levels of government in the United States?

1. ______________________________

2. ______________________________

3. ______________________________

What are the three branches of government in the United States?

4. ______________________________

5. ______________________________

6. ______________________________

What is the only state that has a unicameral legislature?

7. ______________________________

Only two men signed the Declaration of Independence, the Articles of Confederation, and the United States Constitution. One was Robert Morris of Pennsylvania. Who was the other?

8. ______________________________

In what state did this person live after age 22?

9. ______________________________

One way that an American citizen might be asked to serve his country is by being appointed to be the official representative of the United States to another country. This job is called an:

10. ______________________________

Unit 4 Test

Put the letter of the correct answer in the blank beside the number.

_____ 1. The Marine Committee adopted a resolution describing the flag of the United States in:
a. 1777 b. 1787 c. 1797

_____ 2. This President signed the act of Congress that made "The Star-Spangled Banner" our national anthem.
a. George Washington b. Herbert Hoover c. Harry Truman

_____ 3. The Avenue of Flags at Mount Rushmore has this many flags on display:
a. 10 b. 22 c. 56

_____ 4. The Great Seal of the United States features a:
a. dove b. eagle c. turkey

_____ 5. The bird in the previous question holds what kind of branch in one talon?
a. oak b. maple c. olive

_____ 6. The ribbon it holds in its mouth on the Great Seal says:
a. Don't Tread on Me b. United States of America c. E Pluribus Unum

_____ 7. This song, mentioned in an opera writtin in 1767, says to "mind the music and the step."
a. "Columbia" b. "Anchors Aweigh" c. "Yankee Doodle"

_____ 8. The words to this song, which were written in 1895, praise the "amber waves of grain."
a. "America the Beautiful"
b. "My Country, 'Tis of Thee"
c. "Marine's Hymn"

_____ 9. This song, written by an immigrant in 1938, speaks of America as the "land that I love."
a. "My Country, 'Tis of Thee"
b. "God Bless America"
c. "Battle Hymn of the Republic"

_____ 10. The most important American ideal is:
a. faith in God b. equality of income c. voting

Unit 5 Test

Fill in the blanks.

1-2. Every American who lives in one of the fifty states is represented in Congress by one

____________________________ and two ____________________________.

3. The chief executive of a state is called a ____________________________.

4. The chief executive of a city is called a ____________________________.

5-6. The two states that have produced the most Presidents are ________________________

and ____________________________.

7. Gerald Ford became President when ____________________________ resigned.

8. The inauguration of President ____________________________ in 1997 was the first

to be broadcast live on the Internet.

9-10. There have been two father-and-son sets of Presidents. Their last names are

____________________________ and ____________________________.

Unit 6 Test

Put the letter of the correct answer in the blank beside the number.

_____ 1. The U.S. House of Representatives has 435 of these.

_____ 2. This was once used to keep people from voting and was outlawed by the Twenty-fourth Amendment.

_____ 3. This group was granted citizenship and the right to vote by a law Congress passed in 1924.

_____ 4. A piece of paper that reflects a person's vote

_____ 5. This amendment to the Constitution said that the right to vote could not be denied based on race, skin color, or former condition of servitude.

_____ 6. The Federal government takes one of these every ten years.

_____ 7. A polling place is where people who live in this come to vote.

_____ 8. This amendment to the Constitution gave eighteen-year-olds the right to vote.

_____ 9. A vote by the people about a particular issue

_____ 10. The right to vote

a. precinct

b. census

c. district

d. Twenty-sixth

e. Fifteenth

f. ballot

g. Native Americans

h. suffrage

i. referendum

j. poll tax

Unit 7 Test

Indicate whether each statement is true or false.

________ 1. The ticket is the document that states a party's stands or beliefs on various issues.

________ 2. A closed primary only allows registered members of a political party to participate.

________ 3. Someone who attends a convention to participate in the decision-making is called a deputy.

________ 4. The 1968 Democratic National Convention took place during the Vietnam War.

________ 5. The keynote address is the location of the main meeting of convention delegates.

________ 6. Nebraska is the first state to allow voters to express their preference among presidential candidates.

________ 7. Vermont holds the first presidential primary in an election year.

________ 8. A national convention is a meeting held by a political party to nominate a presidential candidate.

________ 9. The Republican Party began in the mid-1850s and held its first national convention in 1856.

________ 10. Andrew Johnson is considered the father of the Democratic Party, which held its first national convention in 1818.

Unit 8 Test

Put the letter of the correct answer in the blank beside the number.

_____ 1. The job of speechwriter for a presidential candidate is usually filled by a:

a. hired staff member b. volunteer c. convention delegate

_____ 2. The press secretary for a presidential candidate is a:

a. volunteer b. precinct worker c. hired staff member

_____ 3. Stuffing envelopes to mail out on behalf of a presidential candidate is work that is usually done by a:

a. hired staff member b. volunteer c. Secret Service agent

_____ 4. Campaigning door-to-door for a presidential candidate is usually done by a:

a. volunteer b. hired staff member c. candidate's family member

_____ 5. Candidates spend money on television, radio, and newspaper:

a. interviews b. editorial opinions c. advertisements

_____ 6. Ronald Reagan used the campaign slogan, "It's ___________ Again in America."

a. Election-Time b. Morning c. Warm

_____ 7. Jimmy Carter's campaign slogan was, "A ________ for a Change."

a. Call b. Democrat c. Leader

_____ 8. Calvin Coolidge's campaign urged voters to "Keep ________ with Coolidge."

a. Going b. Steady c. Cool

_____ 9. The setting in which candidates appear on the same stage, answer questions about their ideas, and respond to each other's answers is called a presidential:

a. decorum b. debate c. debacle

_____ 10. Popular sites for the events described in the previous question are:

a. universities b. sports stadiums c. movie theaters

Unit 9 Test

Indicate whether each statement is true or false.

________ 1. Election officials must purchase equipment and get printed materials ready before Election Day.

________ 2. The Federal agency that decides what places must provide election materials in languages other than English is the U.S. Citizenship and Immigration Services.

________ 3. Election materials are provided in English and a total of three other languages in the U.S.

________ 4. Presidential election results were once sent by the Pony Express.

________ 5. Election results are reported by newspapers and radio.

________ 6. Since television is so influential, television networks do not report election results.

________ 7. The Electoral College refers to the group of people who cast the final votes for President and Vice President.

________ 8. The total number of electors from all fifty states and the District of Columbia is 538.

________ 9. To be elected, a presidential candidate must receive a minimum of 260 electoral votes.

________ 10. The Government Accountability Office is the Federal agency that helps the incoming President make the transition into his new job.

Unit 10 Test

Put the letter of the correct answer in the blank beside the number.

_____ 1. Fled Washington, D.C., during the War of 1812

_____ 2. First President to live in the White House

_____ 3. Cast the bell for St. John's Episcopal Church

_____ 4. University founded to teach deaf and hearing impaired students

_____ 5. System that was abandoned after railroads became important

_____ 6. Hotel of Presidents

_____ 7. National Cemetery located in this city

_____ 8. District of Columbia is located on this river

_____ 9. Jefferson hired him to work on the Capitol

_____ 10. Asked the Federal government to have land returned to it from the District of Columbia

a. Willard

b. Gallaudet

c. Revere

d. Potomac

e. Adams

f. Latrobe

g. Madison

h. Virginia

i. Arlington

j. Canal

Unit 11 Test

Put the letter of the correct answer in the blank beside the number.

_____ 1. The President is the head of the _______________ branch of the Federal government.

a. executive b. legislative c. judicial

_____ 2. As the highest official representative of our country to other countries, the President is:

a. Chief Ambassador b. head of state c. chief of protocol

_____ 3. The President's role as leader of our nation's military forces is called being:

a. Supreme General b. Chief of Staff c. Commander in Chief

_____ 4. The President's annual message to Congress is called the:

a. Annual Report b. State of the Union c. Congressional Message

_____ 5. Subject to the Senate's approval, the President appoints Ambassadors and:

a. Federal Senators b. Federal Park Rangers c. Federal judges

_____ 6. Removing a convicted person's penalty altogether is called a presidential:

a. pardon b. reprieve c. commutation

_____ 7. The President often hosts a foreign head of state at a White House:

a. honorary luncheon b. diplomatic luminary c. state dinner

_____ 8. Any plane carrying the President is designated as:

a. Commander One b. Air Force One c. Military One

_____ 9. The President whose activities on November 30, 1989 are described in Lesson 53 was:

a. Bill Clinton b. Jimmy Carter c. George H. W. Bush

_____ 10. The heads of the executive departments, including State, Defense, and Homeland Security, are members of the President's:

a. Cabinet b. Council of Advisors c. Staff

Unit 12 Test

Indicate whether each statement is true or false.

________ 1. First Lady Lady Bird Johnson promoted the beautification of the American landscape.

________ 2. Thomas Jefferson's home is named Monticello, which is Italian for little river.

________ 3. First Lady Dolley Madison was an excellent hostess.

________ 4. The White House has three bathrooms and 35 elevators.

________ 5. First Lady Hillary Clinton was elected as a U.S. Senator, was appointed Secretary of State, and was the Democratic nominee for President in 2016.

________ 6. The people who help the President and his family are called the cabinet staff.

________ 7. First Lady Jacqueline Kennedy had an interest in historic preservation that was especially displayed through her remodeling of the White House.

________ 8. Thomas Jefferson got many ideas for his home while serving as Ambassador to great Britain.

________ 9. First Lady Rosalynn Carter encouraged the compassionate treatment of those with mental illness.

________ 10. Thomas Jefferson made copies of letters as he wrote them by using a machine called a simulgraph.

Unit 13 Test

Complete these statements with the correct answers.

1. The U.S. House of Representatives and U.S. Senate meet in the building called the United States ______________________ (be sure to spell it correctly!).

2. Members of the House of Representatives serve ______-year terms.

3. U.S. Senators are elected to ______-year terms.

4. There are ________________ members of the United States Senate.

5. There are ________________ members of the U.S. House of Representatives

6. ________-____________ (fraction) of the U.S. Senate is up for election every two years.

7. Senators and Congressmen are appointed to small groups called ______________________ to consider bills that are submitted by the members.

8. When a Congressman introduces a bill, the _________________ of the House assigns it to a committee.

9. If a bill passes the House and Senate in different forms, a ________________________ committee must come up with a version that will be acceptable to both houses.

10. After a bill passes Congress, the President can either sign it, _______________ it, or do nothing.

Unit 14 Test

Put the letter of the correct answer in the blank beside the number.

_____ 1. A key staff member for a member of Congress is the ______________________, who manages interaction with the media.
a. chief of staff b. director of communications c. scheduler

_____ 2. A ______________ helps citizens deal with Federal agencies.
a. legislative aide b. receptionist c. caseworker

_____ 3. The Congressional staffer who meets with lobbyists is the ______________.
a. legislative assistant b. caseworker c. chief of staff

_____ 4. One of the jobs on Capitol Hill is that of the ______________________, who is responsible for taking care of the Capitol Complex.
a. Capitol Chairman
b. Architect of the Capitol
c. Conservator of the Capitol

_____ 5. The Vice President is ________________ of the Senate.
a. President b. Vice President c. Speaker

_____ 6. The Vice President's address is:
a. Number One Observatory Circle
b. Number Two Pennsylvania Avenue
c. 1776 Constitution Avenue

_____ 7. The Vice President's Ceremonial Office is located in the:
a. Library of Congress
b. U.S. Naval Observatory
c. Eisenhower Executive Office Building

_____ 8. In 1800 Congress set aside $5,000 to start a ___________________ that became the Library of Congress.
a. collection of papers b. collection of books c. collection of debates

_____ 9. The three Library of Congress buildings are named for:
a. Washington, Adams, and Lincoln
b. Adams, Cleveland, and Polk
c. Adams, Jefferson, and Madison

_____ 10. "America's Photographer," who is donating thousands of photographs to the Library of Congress, is:
a. Carol Jefferson b. Carol Highsmith c. Carol Douglass

Unit 15 Test

Fill in the blanks with the correct answers.

1. When two countries establish diplomatic relations, they exchange these official representatives: ______________________________

2. This person lives in a foreign country and helps people from his or her home country when they visit: ______________________________

3. This organization was formed after World War II to give countries a place to talk over their differences before starting to fight each other and to bring about better lives for all of the world's citizens: ______________________________

4. Woodrow Wilson traveled to this European nation to take part in the Paris Peace Conference after World War I: ______________________________

5. In 1943 Franklin Roosevelt visited this Africa nation that was begun as a refuge for people who had once been slaves: ______________________________

6. Lyndon Johnson visited this down-under continent-nation in 1966 on his trip that also took him to Vietnam: ______________________________

7. Richard Nixon visited this large Communist country in Asia in 1972: ______________________________

8. This country, America's neighbor to the north, has a maple leaf on its flag: ______________________________

9. This country, known as the "Land of the Rising Sun," was our enemy during World War II but is now an ally. Its flag has a large red circle on a white background: ______________________________

10. This Muslim country in the Middle East has a crescent moon and a star on its flag (hint—it is also the name of a popular Thanksgiving meat dish): ___________________

Unit 16 Test

What are the four branches of the United States military?

1. ______________________________

2. ______________________________

3. ______________________________

4. ______________________________

5. Andrew Jackson, Zachary Taylor, and Dwight Eisenhower were all ______________ in the United States Army.

6. George Washington instructed Thaddeus Kosciusko to design a fortress at __________ ___________ on the Hudson River in New York.

7. President ____________________ signed the legislation that established the United States Military Academy.

8. As superintendent after World War I, General Douglas ________________ emphasized physical fitness at the United States Military Academy.

9. The first-year cadets at the United States Military Academy are called _____________.

10. The Crucible, a three-day intense exercise that concludes basic training, is carried out for recruits in what branch of the U.S. military? ____________________

Unit 17 Test

1-3. Circle three typical state government departments in the names below.

Health	Recreation	Traffic Control
Defense	Education	Transportation
Agriculture	Corrections	Veterans Affairs

4-6. Match the name of the correct city with the states listed.

4. ______ Montana

5. ______ Hawaii

6. ______ Iowa

a. Carson City

b. Honolulu

c. Des Moines

d. Helena

7. (Circle the correct word in each of these two sentences.)

The word capitol refers to a building/city.

The word capital refers to a building/city.

8-9. Five jobs are listed. Circle two jobs that a Governor does.

Appoints a police chief

Attends a political barbecue

Visits troops in Afghanistan

Visits foreign countries on a trade mission

Gives a State of the Union speech

10. What has letters and numbers for identification, is placed on a car, has to be purchased by a car owner, and can be a mini-billboard for a state?

____

Unit 18 Test

Fill in the blanks using the Word Bank below.

1. About 3,000 ___________ exist within the fifty United States today.

2. A typical elected representative in county government is the _____________________.

3. Collecting taxes and paying bills are jobs usually performed by the county _______________.

4. A city begins when it receives a _____________ from the state government.

5. Another term for starting a city is _________________________.

6. The headquarters of city government is the _______________________.

7. The headquarters of county government is the _________________________.

8. In many cities, the person who runs the daily work of the city government is a professional _______________________, who is hired by the city council.

9. In Lesson 88, many people in the community worked together to erect a _________________________.

10. A local ____________________ is a way many communities celebrate their heritage, history, industry, or agriculture.

Word Bank

city hall	festival	treasurer
city manager	stop sign	commissioner
counties	charter	county courthouse
	incorporation	

Unit 19 Test

Multiple Choice. Put the letter of the correct answer in the blank to the left of the number.

_____ 1. The Federal agency that is responsible for carrying out laws regarding Native Americans is the Bureau of:
a. Indian Management b. Indian Affairs c. Indian Heritage

_____ 2. A leader in U.S. relations with Native Americans was:
a. Ely S. Parker b. Andrew Johnson c. Dan Akee

_____ 3. In 1923 Pueblo Indians visited Washington, D.C., bringing a cane given to their tribe by:
a. George Washington b. Andrew Jackson c. Abraham Lincoln

_____ 4. The state with the greatest number of Native Americans is:
a. Tennessee b. California c. Delaware

_____ 5. The capital city of the Navajo Nation is:
a. Window Rock, AZ b. Red River, SD c. Menominee, TX

_____ 6. The Navajo who created a code for the Army during World War II are called:
a. Red Rocks b. Code Talkers c. Navajo Council

_____ 7. The Native American who developed a written language for the Cherokee and whose statue is in National Statuary Hall is:
a. Winnemucca b. Po'pay c. Sequoyah

_____ 8. The Native American who served as a translator for Lewis and Clark and whose statue is in National Statuary Hall is:
a. Wakashie b. Sakakawea c. Will Rogers

_____ 9. The state listed below that does NOT have over 100,000 Native Americans living in it is:
a. Alaska b. New Mexico c. Vermont

_____ 10. The annual period proclaimed by the Federal government for honoring American Indians is called:
a. Native American Heritage Month
b. American Indian Appreciation Week
c. Tribal Honor and Celebration Time

Unit 20 Test

Write the correct acronym of a Federal agency beside its description. Underlined words in the descriptions provide clues to the identity of the agencies.

USCIS FEMA TSA CBP ICE

__________ 1. This Administration provides security for the nation's transportation system, especially air travel.

__________ 2. This agency provides enforcement of laws dealing with customs and immigration.

__________ 3. This Federal agency provides management of the government response to emergency situations.

__________ 4. This agency of the U.S. government provides services related to citizenship and immigration.

__________ 5. This agency provides customs protection at our borders.

Fill in the blanks using the word bank below.

6. The Secret Service is best known for protecting the ____________________.

7. The Secret Service also investigates ________________________.

8. Someone becoming a U.S. citizen must take an oath of allegiance to the U.S. __________________.

9. A new citizen must be able to read, write, and speak basic _______________.

10. A new citizen must show a basic understanding of U.S. history and __________________.

Word Bank

Government counterfeiting English Constitution President

Unit 21 Test

Matching. Match the initials with the proper descriptions.

_____ 1. The state where the first 9-1-1 call was made

_____ 2. This state has a high average annual rainfall.

_____ 3. The State Patrol patch for this state (known for peanuts and Jimmy Carter) is in the shape of the state.

_____ 4. This state is home to the Valley Emergency Communications Center.

_____ 5. This state has a high average of sunny days.

_____ 6. Initials of the man who invented the telephone and made the first emergency call in 1876

_____ 7. This state has frequent hurricanes.

_____ 8. This state's Highway Patrol patch is a triangle and features four Presidents' faces.

_____ 9. This state has frequent serious tornadoes.

_____ 10. This first responder receives about 150 hours of training.

A. OK (Oklahoma)

B. GA (Georgia)

C. AGB

D. SD (South Dakota

E. AL (Alabama)

F. FL (Florida)

G. EMT

H. UT (Utah)

I. HI (Hawaii)

J. AZ (Arizona)

Unit 22 Test

Multiple choice. Put the letter of the correct answer in the blank.

_____ 1. The group of people who listen to the evidence and give a verdict in a court case is the:
a. bailiff　　b. jury　　c. bar

_____ 2. A person who is accused of committing a crime is called the:
a. defendant　　b. attorney　　c. witness

_____ 3. A person who tells personal knowledge about a case is called a:
a. clerk　　b. witness　　c. gavel

_____ 4. The person who is in charge of what happens in a courtroom is the:
a. bailiff　　b. sheriff　　c. judge

_____ 5. Laws are divided into two kinds--civil and:
a. material　　b. legal　　c. criminal

_____ 6. Chuck Colson worked as Special Counsel for President:
a. Nixon　　b. Kennedy　　c. Carter

_____ 7. The office and hotel complex that was the site of a burglary which led to a scandal is the:
a. Rivergate　　b. Watergate　　c. Willowgate

_____ 8. After he left prison, Chuck Colson formed a ministry called:
a. Prison Freedom　　b. Prison Roundtable　　c. Prison Fellowship

_____ 9. The program that provides gifts for the children of people in prison is called:
a. Angel Tree　　b. Christmas Charity　　c. Children's Hope

_____ 10. The U.S. Supreme Court currently has how many justices?
a. 3　　b. 6　　c. 9

Unit 23 Test

Complete these statements using the Word Bank below. Not all words in the Word Bank will be used.

1. The tax that is added to the purchase price of a product is the ____________________.

2. Moving products from one location to another is called ____________________.

3. The money that a bank pays to customers when they deposit their money in the bank is called ____________________.

4. The letter and number combinations such as K 11, D 4, and A 1 designate ____.

5. The greatest source of revenue for the Federal government is the personal ______________________.

6. In 2011 ______________________ by the Federal government was greater than its ________________.

Word Bank

sales tax	distribution	revenue	penalty
excise tax	consumption	spending	circulation
income tax	Federal Reserve Banks	interest	socialism

7-10. Put these four steps of making flour from wheat in the order that they occur.

bagging growing milling harvesting

7. ______________ 8. ______________ 9. ______________ 10. ______________

Unit 24 Test

Multiple choice. Put the letter of the correct answer in the blank.

_____ 1. Hoover Dam is located in the Colorado River between Nevada and:
a. Arizona b. Ohio c. Colorado

_____ 2. The state that produces the most coal in the U.S. is:
a. Florida b. Wyoming c. Delaware

_____ 3. The state that produces the second-highest output of oil in the U.S. is:
a. North Dakota b. California c. Tennessee

_____ 4. New Mexico is a good place to produce electricity from:
a. rain b. sunlight c. dense forests

_____ 5. Solar power and geothermal energy are considered:
a. renewable b. illegal c. unhealthy

_____ 6. Hydroelectricity is produced by:
a. coal heating natural gas
b. sunlight turning the blades on windmills
c. water turning turbines in dams on rivers

_____ 7. Nuclear power
a. is not used in the United States
b. produces some electricity in the United States
c. always gives off large amounts of harmful radioactive emissions

_____ 8. The Roscoe Wind Farm is located in:
a. Alaska b. North Carolina c. Texas

_____ 9. The price for farm products that the government determines to be fair is called:
a. parity b. equity c. surplus

_____ 10. A fuel that is often made from corn is:
a. corybutal b. methane c. ethanol

Unit 25 Test

Matching. Put the letter of the correct answer in the blank to the left of the number.

_____ 1. Oversees most international mail

_____ 2. Invented the "flyer" or airplane

_____ 3. Launched and landed the Space Shuttle

_____ 4. Invented the reaper

_____ 5. First Postmaster General

_____ 6. Invented the telephone

_____ 7. Software pioneer

_____ 8. Source of news and information about America for people in other countries

_____ 9. He and his associates invented the automatic switchboard and the rotary dial telephone.

_____ 10. Invented a device that recorded the human voice

A. Thomas Edison

B. Bill Gates

C. Cyrus McCormick

D. VOA

E. Wright Brothers

F. UPU

G. Almon Strowger

H. Alexander Graham Bell

I. Benjamin Franklin

J. NASA

Unit 26 Test

Complete these statements using the Word Bank at the bottom of the page. Not all of the words in the Word Bank will be used.

1. The welcome signs in ____________________ have words in English and French.

2. The southernmost point in the continental United States is in ________________.

3. The world's first major runway built entirely offshore is in _________________.

4. Roadways are designed by ___________ engineers.

5. Many roadways are made with ________________.

6. Subways, buses, and elevated trains are examples of ____________________.

7. A ____________________________ helps keep school children safe.

8. An ____ helps plans take off and land safely.

9. A ______________________ driver steers big rigs on highways.

10. A __________________ engineer drives trains.

Word Bank

Texas	crossing guard	asphalt
tractor-trailer	interstate commerce	Florida
air traffic controller	Alabama	locomotive
Hawaii	sawdust	civil
Louisiana	mass transit	semi-hauler

Unit 27 Test

Put the letter of the correct answer in the blank to the left of the number.

_____ 1. This work began in England in the 1780s to teach children who worked six days a week.

_____ 2. This Federal program funds food and nutritional education for expectant women, mothers, and young children.

_____ 3. This Federal agency helps people buy a home with a lower than usual down payment.

_____ 4. This Federal program provides a minimum level of income for retired persons.

_____ 5. This program provides health care for the elderly.

_____ 6. William Booth began this ministry in London in 1852.

_____ 7. This Federal agency began in 1912.

_____ 8. This Federal executive department oversees about 300 programs.

_____ 9. This program, which replaced the food stamp program, helps low income families with purchasing food.

_____ 10. This private organization helps low- to moderate-income families own their own home.

A. The Salvation Army

B. Children's Bureau

C. Health and Human Services

D. Supplemental Nutrition Assistance Program (SNAP)

E. Sunday school

F. Women, Infants, and Children (WIC)

G. Habitat for Humanity

H. Social Security

I. Federal Housing Administration

J. Medicare

Unit 28 Test

Multiple choice. Put the letter of the correct answer in the blank.

_____ 1. The college Theodore Roosevelt attended was:

a. Yale b. Princeton c. Harvard

_____ 2. Roosevelt owned property in the ___________ Territory.

a. Wisconsin b. Dakota c. Wyoming

_____ 3. During his childhood, Roosevelt suffered from:

a. tuberculosis b. food allergies c. asthma

_____ 4. The first state to require children to attend school was:

a. Massachusetts b. Pennsylvania c. South Carolina

_____5. The legislation that helped World War II veterans attend college was the:

a. Smoot-Hawley Act b. College Benefit Law c. G. I. Bill

_____ 6. Public schools that do not have to follow typical rules and regulations are called:

a. integrated schools b. charter schools c. released schools

_____ 7. The Corn Palace is located in:

a. South Dakota b. Iowa c. Kansas

_____ 8. The Georgia O'Keeffe Museum is located in:

a. Kansas b. Florida c. New Mexico

_____ 9. A (An) _________________ is like an opera with a Biblical subject.

a. charango b. oratorio c. desoto

_____ 10. *Nutcracker* and *Swan Lake* are compositions in the category of:

a. ballet b. symphony c. recital

Unit 29 Test

Multiple choice. Put the letter of the correct answer in the blank.

_____ 1. The largest state park in the United States is:

a. Yellowstone Park b. Adirondack Park c. Brandywine Creek State Park

_____ 2. To preserve a President's home, Ann Pamela Cunningham founded the:

a. Mount Vernon Ladies' Association b. Monticello Dames c. Hermitage Society

_____ 3. The list of places recognized as worthy of preservation is the:

a. Federal Historic House List
b. American History Association
c. National Register of Historic Places

_____ 4. Plimoth Plantation is a:

a. living history museum b. marketplace museum c. preservation place

_____ 5. George Washington created the Badge of Military Merit at:

a. Mount Vernon b. Philadelphia c. Hasbrouck House

_____ 6. The "Hotel of Presidents" is the nickname of the:

a. Hasbrouck House b. Willard Hotel c. Red Roof Inn

_____ 7. The United States Postal Service honors history by issuing:

a. articles about Presidents b. warnings about vandals c. commemorative stamps

_____ 8. Many state parks were built in the 1930s by the:

a. Federal State Park Authority
b. Civilian Conservation Corps
c. U.S. Corps of Engineers

_____ 9. In 1860 the operations at Mount Vernon were taken over by the:

a. Mount Vernon Ladies' Association
b. Virginia Dames Society
c. Washington Family Trust

_____ 10. The oldest state park in the U.S. is:

a. Boston Heritage State Park b. Niagara Falls State Park c. Liberty State Park

Unit 30 Test

Match the descriptions with the correct names or positions.

_____ 1. Elected to his or her position, sometimes interested in running for higher office

_____ 2. Helps people talk to each other when they don't speak the same language

_____ 3. Often gives a speech at a local ceremony

_____ 4. Explains to a jury their responsibility

_____ 5. Represents his country in another country

_____ 6. These served as Chief Justices of the U.S. Supreme Court.

_____ 7. Served in the U. S. House (before the Civil War) and U.S. Senate (after the Civil War) from Mississippi

_____ 8. Served as Secretary of State under Harry Truman

_____ 9. These served in the U.S. House of Representatives.

_____ 10. How we might summarize the lessons of *Uncle Sam and You*

A. John Marshall, Salmon P. Chase, and Fred Vinson

B. James F. Byrnes

C. Ambassador

D. Governor

E. judge

F. Lucius Quintus Cincinnatus Lamar II

G. Love your neighbor as yourself.

H. mayor

I. interpreter

J. John Marshall, L.Q. C. Lamar II, James Byrnes, and Fred Vinson

Image Credits

Numbers indicate the page numbers of images. The meanings of the letters t, m, b, l, and r are as follows: t - top of page; m - middle; b - bottom; l - left; r - right.

Images marked CC-BY-2.0 are licensed through the Creative Commons Attribution 2.0 Generic License. For more information, visit http://creativecommons.org/licenses/by/2.0/deed.en

Aaron/robinsonsmay (Flickr, CC-BY-2.0), 81
Andrew Magill/AMagill (Flickr, CC-BY-2.0), 82
Architect of the Capitol, 37, 51, 53, 54
Arian Zwegers (Flickr, CC-BY-2.0), 46
Bethany Poore, 2, 3, 31b, 84 (map), 90 (map), 93 (map)
Carl Malamud (Flickr, CC-BY-2.0), 65
Carol M. Highsmith's America, Library of Congress, 1, 113
Charlene Notgrass, 112b
CIA World Factbook, 57, 60
Cliff1066™ (Flickr, CC-BY-2.0), 20b, 61
cogdogblog (Flickr, CC-BY-2.0), 48, 56
Fort Wainright Public Affairs Office (Flickr, CC-BY-2.0), 76 #4
George H. W. Bush Presidential Library, 43
Grand Canyon NPS (Flickr, CC-BY-2.0), 76 (#2, #3, #5, #6, #7, #8), 80 (Michael Quinn)
JaxStrong (Flickr, CC-BY-2.0), 55
Jim Bowen/jimbowen0306 (Flickr, CC-BY-2.0), 66 (Des Moines)
John Notgrass, 79
kansasphoto (Flickr, CC-BY-2.0), 78
Kate Ure/kanu101 (Flickr, CC-BY-2.0), 66 (Honolulu)
katerha (Flickr, CC-BY-2.0), 40
KOMUnews (Flickr, CC-BY-2.0), 70
Library of Congress, 19, 22, 23, 24, 28, 30, 31t, 34, 36
markn3tel (Flickr, CC-BY-2.0), 50
muffet (Flickr, CC-BY-2.0), 21
Oregon Department of Transportation/OregonDOT (Flickr, CC-BY-2.0), 67
Ryan Wick (Flickr, CC-BY-2.0), 66 (Madison)
teofilo (Flickr, CC-BY-2.0), 66 (Carson City)
Tracy Elizabeth (Flickr, CC-BY-2.0), 66 (Helena)
U.S. Army (Flickr, CC-BY-2.0), 42
U.S. Army Corps of Engineers, Norfolk District/norfolkdistrict (Flickr, CC-BY-2.0), 76 (#1, #9 - U.S. Army Photos by Patrick Bloodgood)
U.S. Department of State (Flickr, CC-BY-2.0), 45
U.S. Senate Collection, 20t
Wikimedia Commons, 58, 63, 109
wmrice (Flickr, CC-BY-2.0), 25

All other images from JupiterImages.